WAR IS HELL

8-2016

DEAR BUD —

I HOPE YOU ENJOY

MY LITTLE BOOK.

MILT ——

Milton A. Rhea

Printed in Victoria, Canada

A cataloguing record for this book that includes the U.S. Library of Congress Classification number, the Library of Congress Call number and the Dewey Decimal cataloguing code is available from the National Library of Canada. The complete cataloguing record can be obtained from the National Library's online database at: www.nlc-bnc.ca/amicus/index-e.html
ISBN: 1-4120-1716-5

TRAFFORD

This book was published _on-demand_ in cooperation with Trafford Publishing. On-demand publishing is a unique process and service of making a book available for retail sale to the public taking advantage of on-demand manufacturing and Internet marketing. **On-demand publishing** includes promotions, retail sales, manufacturing, order fulfilment, accounting and collecting royalties on behalf of the author.

Suite 6E, 2333 Government St., Victoria, B.C. V8T 4P4, CANADA
Phone   250-383-6864   Toll-free 1-888-232-4444 (Canada & US)
Fax   250-383-6804   E-mail   sales@trafford.com
Web site www.trafford.com TRAFFORD PUBLISHING IS A DIVISION OF TRAFFORD HOLDINGS LTD.
Trafford Catalogue #03-2093   www.trafford.com/robots/03-2093.html

10   9   8   7   6   5   4

War is Hell

The lasting impressions of a young sailor's
war and for those shipmates that cried because
of the blood shed and the tears from the salt water
in their eyes ~ I'm proud to be one of you.

Milton A Rhea

"Now hear this"

This little book would not have happened if it were not for
the guiding hands of my editor Maxine Atchison and the
love and encouragement of my wonderful wife, Ruby

TO THE READER

You will be moved by this tale. It may bring tears to your
eyes as it did to mine as you are absorbed into the
tribulations of one American sailor who survived the Pacific
naval campaigns of World War II. It will amuse you as you
walk in the footsteps of a young man in unfamiliar territory.
and it will give you insight through the eyes of a warrior
who personally experienced one of the great moments of
human history. It is told frankly and its authenticity is
enhanced with bits of contemporary vernacular and
accounts of numerous unsanctioned, but relatively

harmless, escapades.

War really is hell. The millions of stories that are told by those who went to battle, those who stayed behind, those that didn't come back and those who suffered its ravages as it passed through, testify to its

heavy impact on our global history. Collectively, their sorrow weighs heavily on our hearts. Individually, they are often tales of disaster, portraying dramatic alterations to families that must be reformed to compensate for the missing members.

This story, the saga of a teenager growing up to manhood quickly, far from home, reviews the triumphs, trauma and unique insights that can only be revealed by one who was an integral part of the day to day struggles of a massive war. It tells about the feelings, the actions, the problems and even some bits of humor in these horrifying, exciting and dangerous missions across the Pacific Ocean during World War II. It sketches the experiences of a brave young decorated sailor routinely risking life itself while intimately involved in frantic naval warfare. This tale ended with the job completed and a safe trip home.

It wasn't so for many others. But this story has one more facet that makes it particularly poignant. This young sailor who personally faced the hazards of the Pacific campaign in the 1940's, later married, and had two sons. As you will discover in reading this saga, this family knows the risks, trauma and sorrows of war in a very real way. Now, his grandsons will

know These issues as well and we trust because of this, they will be better citizens of our world.

Unfortunately, stories such as this will continue to be experienced, documented and relived by those who are summoned to solve the world's problems in this manner. When we eventually find a better way of resolving our global differences, such stories need no longer be written. They will only be a part of our history and folklore, like tales of the sea told by old salts.

Pray for that day. ~ Charles Atchison
A nephew and huge fan of the author

Randy and Casey, My wonderful Grandsons

The following is a collection of sea stories. They were
events covering about three years of my life (18
trough 21 years of age) as a young man. I can proudly say
that I was totally involved in one of the major events in our
country's history.
Some day, one of your children may be studying

American history and find it interesting that his/her great-
grandfather took part in this all- encompassing war.

It is very difficult to talk about the realities of war;
however, defending your country and your way of life is
worth fighting for, and even dying for. On the other hand, it
certainly seems we should find a better way to solve the
differences between nations other than   sending
productive young men to experience the   horrors of
war, which include mental breakdowns, pain, suffering and
often times death! It appears that our military leaders must

command some sort of "death defying struggle", or all of their lifetime of training would be for nothing. We elect our nation's leaders to negotiate with other countries for the benefit of all mankind, but it seem the power of a strong political position sometimes outweighs the benefit of preserving our youth. Do I sound bitter? You bet I do! Having been there and witnessed war first hand, and having suffered the internal pain of losing a young son (your Uncle Randy) for a useless effort at Viet Nam leaves me with a helpless attitude. I truly love my country and feel very fortunate to be an American,   However, it seems we have learned

nothing from our past experiences and events of history. Three years without home cooking and "soft"

girls. Read on, as I will write about some of the most exciting times in my younger life.

You can believe that the man who came home was   not the same boy who left thirty-four months prior.
My appreciation of country, family and fellow men was set

for life. The Lord answered my prayers and my life was spared. Every day has been a gift to enjoy to the fullest and most of all of my dreams to date have come true.

So I say to you, my wonderful grandsons, put your lives in the hands of God and be kind and thoughtful as everyone is fighting a tough battle.

With much love from your Grandmother and I,

Grandpa Milton

"Now hear this"" ~ All of the names, places, dates and information that follows are embedded in the memory stored in my 80 year old brain, they are not meant to be fiction, they are pretty close but not necessarily accurate ~ so be kind.

A Chronology of Events and the Ships Log

12/18/24	· Happy Birthday to me
12/18/29	· Grammar School
12/18/40	· Our Calculating President
12/07/41	· REMEMBER PEARL HARBOR
12/18/42	· Pacific Disasters
12/18/42	· High School
04/01/43	· I will ~ "GO FORWARD AND CONQUER"
06/05/43	Boot Training, San Diego
06/28/43	· Amphibious Boat Training, San Diego
06/29/43	· Traveled to Oakland.
06/30/43	· COMMISSIONED THE USS PIERCE PA50
07/15/43	· Completed shake down cruise
07/20/43	· San Diego to pick up Higgins landing craft
07/23/43	· Departed to Pearl Harbor
07/25/43	· Liberty in Honolulu
09/01/43	· Drinking the Hard Stuff
10/01/43	· Sailed to Maui for training in boat landings
11/15/43	· Departed for the Gilbert Atoll
11/15/43	· LANDED ON THE BEACH OF MAKIN
11/25/43	· Departed to Pearl Harbor
12/02/43	· Arrived at Pearl Harbor
12/10/43	· Sailed to Maui for more training

01/22/44	· Departed for the Marshall Islands
01/31/44	· LANDED ON THE BEACH OF KWAJALEIN
02/03/44	· THE PIERCE TO THE ROCKY MOUNT
02/25/44	· Departed for Pearl Harbor
03/03/44	· Arrived at Pearl Harbor
05/15/44	. Sailed to Maui for more training
05/19/44	· Left Maui for Pearl Harbor
05/20/44	· Arrived at Pearl Harbor
05/29/44	· Departed for Eniwetok Island, Marshalls
06/8/44	· Arrived at Eniwetok Island to lead invasion
06/11/44	· Departed for Mariana Islands
06/15/44	· LANDED ON THE BEACH AT SAIPAN
06/17/44	· Japan's Naval Fleet approaching.
06/18/44	· FIRST BATTLE OF THE PHILIPPINES (Air)
06/20/44	· Returned to Saipan Island
07/20/44	· Departed for Guam Island
07/21/44	· LANDED ON THE BEACHES OF GUAM
07/23/44	· Departed for Tinian Island
07/24/44	· LANDED ON THE BEACHES OF TINIAN
07/26/44	· Departed for Saipan Island
07/26/44	· Arrived Saipan
08/12/44	· Departed Saipan for Guam Island

08/13/44	· Arrived at Guam
08/15/44	· Departed Guam for Pearl Harbor
08/26/44	· Arrived in Pearl Harbor
09/01/44	· Departed for Maui Island for more training
09/02/44	· Arrived at Maui
09/06/44	· Departed for Pearl Harbor
09/07/44	· Arrived at Pearl Harbor
09/15/44	· Departed for Eniwetok Island
09/25/44	· Arrived at Agnatic in the Marshall Islands
09/07/44	· Departed Agnatic for Manus
09/28/44	· Departed Manus in the Admiralty Islands
10/01/44	· Crossed the Equator, Neptune's initiations
10/03/44	· Arrived at Manus Island
10/14/44	· Time to lead invasion in the Philippines
10/20/44	· Landed on the beach, San Jose, Philippines
10/24/44	· Jap's Fleet approaching from China Sea,
10/25/44	· LANDED ON THE BEACH AT MINDANAO
10/26/44	· Hollandia Islands, Dutch New Guinea
10/27/44	· Arrived at Hollandia Islands
10/28/44	· Departed for Cape Gloucester, New Britain
10/29/44	· Arrived at Cape Gloucester
12/09/44	· Manus Island in the Admiralty Islands

1210/44	· Arrived at Manus Island
12/16/44	· Departed for Lae, British New Guinea
12/18/44	· We lost three destroyers - Cobra Typhoon
12/18/44	· Arrived at Lea
12/20/44	· Departed for Manus Island
12/22/44	· Arrived at Manus Island
12/31/44	· Departed for Luzon, Philippines
01/09/45	· LANDED AT THE LINGAYEN GULF
02/20/45	· Departed for Subic Bay
02/21/45	· Arrived at Subic Bay
02/22/45	· Departed Subic Bay for Mindoro, Philippines
02/23/45	· Arrived at Mindoro
02/24/44	· Departed Mindoro for Tacloban, Leyte Gulf
02/25/45	· Arrived at Tacloban
02/27/45	· Departed for Mindoro, Philippines
02/29/45	· Arrived at Mindoro
03/08/45	· Departed for Samboanga,Mindanao,
03/10/45	·THE BEACH AT ZAMBOANGA
03/24/45	· Departed for Subic Bay
03/26/45	· Arrived at Subic Bay
03/27/45	· Departed for Leyte Gulf
03/31/45	· Arrived at Leyte Gulf

04/04/45	. Departed Leyte for Mortorai & Duch Indies
04/06/45	· Arrived at Morotai
04/07/45	· The invasion of Thyroxin, Borneo
05/01/45	· LANDED ON THE BEACH AT THYROXIN
05/03/45	· Departed for Marathi, Borneo
05/05/45	· Arrived at Marathi
06/04/45	· Departed for Lauan, Brunei Bay, Borneo
06/10/45	· LANDED ON THE BEACH AT BRUNEI BAY
06/17/45	· Departed for Torosa, Leyte Gulf
06/18/45	· Admiral Royal found dead in cabin
06/20/45	· Tolosa /Tacloban for the Admiral's funeral
06/24/45	· Departed Tacloban for Osmena, Samra
06/25/45	· Arrived at Osmena for repairs
08/01/45	. Domei News reported that Japan had accepted the Potsdam Terms

THE WAR IS OVER ~ Ahh Soo WE BEAT THOSE SUCKERS

09/03/45	· Departed for Manila
09/04/45	Arrived at Manila's tent city
09/25/45	· Board an old transport

10/05/45	· Arrived at Seattle Navel Base
10/29/45	· Board train for Los Angeles,
11/01/45	· HOME – (I'M CRYING AS I WRITE THIS)
12/01/45	· Report to Terminal Island Naval Base
01/0?/46	HONORABLE DISCHARGE, Thank you Sir

November 1st 1946 ~ Not a bad looking kid ?

Hello, My name is Milton Rhea

A boatswains Mate 2nd Class

Please, won't you come along with me on a little journey –
from my boyhood to manhood? This is not fiction or is it
the result of a lot of research, It is real life story and It's
from me to you.

From the shores of America to the China Seas, and across
the vast Pacific Ocean, our leaders used the volcanic
peaks as "stepping stones" on our path toward our victory
in World War Two. In so doing, I, and those like me,
changed these idyllic islands and their innocent people ~
we produced a blood bath of human destruction and waste!
Could I, and those like me, have taken a different path to
accomplish the same results?

If you will allow me, I will give you a personal accounting of
what it was like for a young lad, facing peril while walking
on the edge of life itself, and the determination of a man in
the sunset of his life to find the answers.

For the sake of any genealogist out there, I was born
December 18th,1924 in Los Angeles, (Hollywood)
California. My parents were Fred and Florence Rhea who

brought me home to a little house at 3301 London Street in North Los Angeles. My father built this house five years before I was born for my mother my older brother Freddy. At the time I didn't know about depressions. I was just a happy little boy who loved everyone and was loved by all. We raised chickens, rabbits and of course a garden. I do remember Mom dying Dads hair brown so he might find a job. He finally got on the assembly line at Ford Motor Co. in Long Beach. Mom had a life time job as a telephone operator at Robinson's Department Store. I remember so well staying home from school because I had no shoes and Mom sending me to the store with her last quarter (she said I had a way to charm the butcher) to buy a big bone with meat on it for 5 cents and 20 cents worth of mixed vegetables from the Japanese gardener. This would make soup for a week. I would get up early on Saturday mornings and cut the neighbors lawns till I made a dime to see my favorite cowboy Tom Mix at the Rampart theater. Going to school and getting good grades was not very high on my list of what was important and my parents were to busy trying to survive to care. I was what today they call "A street kid". I learned how to survive by being creative on my own time. As long as I stayed out of trouble and lived in my own little world everything was just fine.

Year 1934 – My first experience with the Japanese happened at grammar school one day, a Japanese boy walked up to me and took a ball out of my hands and walked away. I knew this was not a very nice thing for him to do, and I didn't really know what to do about it. However, I also knew it was up to me to make things right. So I picked the boy up and dropped him on his head, picked up my ball and walked away. After he was taken to the hospital, the principal called my mother and suggested that because of a large percentage of the kids in this school were Japanese, it would be wise for her to come get me and take me to a different school, "right now". In junior high we were back together again and I apologized for the scar on his forehead. He apologized for taking my ball and we were buddies thereafter. This experience should have given me a clue as to what was to come.

Summery to Date

Politics Prior to December 7th, and the beginning of WWII

in the Pacific ~ You don't have to do much research to find that President Roosevelt and congress, along with our military leaders were in a pretty tough position. It was a lose-lose situation. Our allies in Europe were losing big time on all fronts, and the submarines were destroying our commercial shipping in the Atlantic. The major commodity to fight a war was oil. Our friends in Europe were running dry, so we had to help out "or else".

We were also getting low on oil resources ourselves, so when President Roosevelt decided to help his old British buddy, Winston Churchill. The only thing Roosevelt could do it seems was to cut off our oil shipments to Japan who depended on the United States for over 80% of their oil to run their country. Japan had only enough oil to last a year. Well, anyone in their right mind could see that Japan's only choice was to move into the South East Asia oil fields to survive. This would make them look like the bad guys and we would have to stop them with all of our battleships and carriers in the Pacific Ocean. After all we ruled the Pacific, so not to worry!

Our intelligence operators picked up a message to the Japanese Ambassador in Germany saying: "To save it's very life, Japan must take immediate steps to break out of this ever strengthening chain of encirclement, which is being woven under the guidance and with the participation of England and the United States, acting like a cunning dragon – seemingly asleep."

"Now Hear This" is a phrase used after blowing my "boatsuns pipe" (an ear splitting whistle) over a ship's speaker system to precede an important announcement. I use it here after to alert the reader.

I will be taking you from the beginning to the end of the Pacific war not as a historian but through the tears of a young sailor trying to understand what our great leaders were doing and why. I will be naming names of some of the very top leaders in the Navy because they were very meaningful in my naval experience. You will read later how I "sort of" became friends with a lot of them.

Vise Admiral Richmond Kelly Turner was in charge of "War

Plans" in Washington DC. He was a very dominating, man who intimidated everyone around him. He was absolutely sure the Japanese were moving their main navel forces down into the South China Seas to capture all the oil land available, and it's true, Japan was doing this. However, at the same time our intelligence operators were reporting to Washington that even though the Japanese Navy was under radio silence, they were picking up reports that a great number of Japanese oil tankers were making their way up towards the North Pacific Ocean. This could only mean there had to be a fleet of Japanese ships up there, somewhere, and the only reason for their presence in that area had to be an attack on Pearl Harbor, United States or Panama Canal. My future boss, Admiral Turner, said he knew the Japanese main forces were in the South China Seas and asked that he not be bothered with a bunch of tankers out in the Pacific. He made no effort to contact Admiral Kimmel in Hawaii. Of course this was one of our country's worst military blunders in our history, and the real beginning of the Pacific Ocean war. President Roosevelt really started it all with the sanctions on Japanese oil. He had to know the consequences of this drastic move and patiently waited for the war to begin.

While our great American leaders were playing guessing games, a Japanese Admiral named Nagumo finally reached the staging area, about 300 miles north of Hawaii, completely undetected. Admiral Nagumo had six carriers, 49 high level bombers, 51 dive-bombers, 40 torpedo planes and 43 escort zero fighters - and this was just the first wave! The second wave had 54 bombers, and 78 dive-bombers. The total Japanese task force that attacked Pearl Harbor was approximately 315 ships and aircraft.

Prime minister Winston Churchill called President Roosevelt and informed him that his intelligence were reporting that the Japanese were planning an attack on Pearl Harbor on December the 7th or 8th. Roosevelt thanked him and said that he would be unavailable during that time. A big mistake Mr. President.   It was obvious that we needed to go to war with Japanese but this was not the way to do it.

12-18-1940

The president's original plan of stationing two old gun boats in the China seas that would surely be sunk by the Japanese fleet in there effort to capture the oil lands in south East Asia thus giving us the right to declare war.

Before you start throwing rocks at me for the above statements take a look at the Congressional Record now available in Washington. It's so sad to see such a great leader who has done so many wonderful things for our country do something so stupid. It's always disappointing to find that great leaders are just people after all.

Remember Pearl Harbor

Corregidor

New Guinea

Solomons

Bataan

Kept in the Dark: Admiral Kimmel and General Short were not informed that the focus of American strategy in the fall of 1941 had shifted from defense based on the Pacific Fleet in Pearl Harbor (below, note prominence of oil storage tanks in upper left) to a strategic bomber deterrent five thousand miles away in the Philippines.

25

DECEMBER 7th 1941

At 7:53 a.m., the Japanese pilots yelled as the dove their planes into our great Naval Base

Pearl Harbor at the island of Hawaii "TORA, TORA, TORA" (Tiger, Tiger, Tiger). They destroyed nine battleships, one heavy cruiser, six light cruisers and many destroyers. Our total port authority and airfields were in shambles. For some unknown reason the Japanese passed up a whole field of oil tanks that would have kept our remaining aircraft carriers, Admiral Halsey and the Enterprise fleet in the Pacific completely helpless without oil.

We lost 2,403 service men (half inside the battleship ARIZONA battleship), 68 civilians and 1,178 wounded. Only 34 out of 400 men entombed in the Battleship OKLAHOMA battleship got out safely.

All of the people on the Hawaiian Islands were In a state of shock; they were not prepared to defend themselves. They were sure that Japan was going to invade the islands but had no idea as to what to do about it.

Just for the record, the Japanese pilots destroyed the following ships: The Detroit, Raleigh, Utah, Tangier, Curtis

Medusa, Blue, Phoenix, Solace, Allen Chaw, Nevada, Vestal, West Virginia, Oklahoma, Arizona, Tennessee, Maryland, Neoshe, California, Avect, Downs, Casein, Pennsylvania, St. Louis, Bagley, Honolulu, San Francisco, New Orleans, Ramepo, Sacramento, Argonne, Helena, Oglala, Cachalot, Shaw, Sumner, Caster, Pelias plus several submarines and mine sweepers. Not a bad morning's work!

This is my own little summary going on here. If you want to get all of the straight facts, purchase the books: "AND I WAS THERE" by Rear Admiral Edwin T. Layton, USN or Lt. Commander, Kenneth Landis USNR book "DECEIT AT PEARL HARBOR'.

I was sixteen years old at the time of Pearl Harbor, and it didn't seem like any big deal to me. I had no concept of the meaning of life and death. I thought that we should send our Los Angeles Police Department over there and lock them all up. I was amazed at how everyone was so concerned. I soon learned that there was serious stuff going on around town and it was beginning to affect my life. No lights at night, no gasoline, tiers, food was getting tough to find, everyone was planting "Victory" gardens and all sorts of uncomfortable things to remember that had the "War Effort" attached to it.

12-18-1942

One day at high school, there was a special assembly in our auditorium and we were informed that all of our Japanese students were going to be moved to camps out in the desert.

We had just elected a Japanese student body president who informed us that "Everything was just fine". He knew this was good for the country and in a little while they would be back in class. He had no idea just how unfair he and the local American Japanese communities were going to be treated. I thought it was terrible, but at the same time I also knew my Japanese friends were quietly taking afternoon classes in Japanese language and our school president was a black belt in Judo training.

At our 50 year high school class reunion a special effort was made to invite our Japanese students and it was wonderful to see them again especially a tiny little girl (woman) that did all of my home work for me. I think she had a crush on me because she really blushed as only a Japanese girl can. But I think everyone was a little uncomfortable, There had been to much pain and frustration to erase the obvious.

I must say something important at this time. I and most of the people I know have the greatest respect for the Japanese people. I know them as kind, gentle and thoughtful people. But among their race there were some animals that brought the worst kind of pain and unnecessary suffering to the American troops. It is this element that I here after refer to as "JAPS'".

It was really nice to see some of my old girl friends. Some of them gave me a knowing smile. It was great to see my old football buddies too. Some of my old teachers broke every rule in the books to get me a high school diploma.

30

While I was fighting the battle of Belmont High School there were several sea battles that were going on so I must mention them to keep a proper perspective going on what is going on here.

February 22nd 1941 – The Philippians

The Japanese now had free run of the whole Pacific, so the first order of business for Japan was to move into the Philippines. The main invasion landed in Lingayen Gulf and several other points within a week. Our complete Army Air Force stationed on the islands was wiped out on the ground in just one half-hour. General MacArthur knew they were coming, and let it happen. No one has been able to figure that one out yet. The American Army suffered its biggest defeat in history when Bataan fell on April 9, 1941. After leaving his troops in the Philippines, General MacArthur took his wife, dog and some personal things and sailed for Australia in a PT Boat .and then transferred to a submarine because he was so sea sick.   Later, General MacArthur made an effort to recapture some of the

islands in Guadalcanal, the Solomons and New Guinea as stair steps back to his beloved Philippines. This was some of our most difficult fighting in very hot, slimy weather and a muddy jungle landscape.

April 18th1942 ~ We bomb Japan

Admiral Halsey sent General Doolittle to bomb Japan's mainland from a carrier in our first attempt to show our strength. Four airmen were lost in crash landings in China, and three were executed in Tokyo.

May5th,1942 ~ The Battle of the Coral Sea

The battle of the Coral Sea was the first major battle where the opposing ships were never in sight of each other. We lost our precious carrier, LEXINGTON. Both sides had tremendous losses, but the U. S. Navy came out on top by letting Admiral Yamamoto know he had "awakened the sleeping giant"!

June 6th 1942 ~ The Battle of Midway

The battle of Midway ended as a glorious victory for our
Navy in statistics. We did turn away the invasion of
Midway, but our losses were overwhelming. We lost 347
lives, a carrier, a destroyer and 147 aircraft. The
Japanese lost four carriers, one cruiser, 2,500 men and
322 aircraft. Can you imagine the terror that most of those
Japanese pilots felt when they saw their ship go down with
no place to land. They were the cream of the crop, the
most experienced in their air force. This was a tremendous
loss to the Japanese Navy.

June 3rd 1942 ~ Alaska/Aleutian ~ A Separate War

The 34,000 mile coastline is part of the United States but it
was mostly unexplored with only a few old Russian maps
Most of the time this frozen wasteland was covered with a

dense fog and ice and nearly impossible to defend or invade. Alaska was part of the Western Defense Council with no military communications, no Air Corp. planes or landing fields Later on our General Buckner had about 800 troops and a few armed civilians.

Alaska had one 1867 cannon that was being used as a flower pot. It was August 12th 1940 congress sent 350 million and we had an obsolete Martin B-10 and a small civilian airport. By 1941 we had PBY Catalinas to patrol the Aleutian sky when it wasn't fogged over

June 5th 1941 Finally, Japan made an effort to bomb Duch Harbor and we lost 750,000 gallons of fuel and 18 lives. so our war in the north pacific with Japan really began.

June 7th 1942 After taking the islands of Attu and Kiska with 2500 crack combat Japanese troops the Pacific war in Alaska and the Aleutian Islands we really got down to the business of fighting a war. On May 11,1943 we took back our islands. We lost 516 troops with 1,136 wounded. The Jap's lost 2,150 . Of course I wasn't there so it would be worth while reading "The Thousand Mile War" by Brian Garfield. Considering all of the negative physical and weather conditions our troops and air force made a super human effort in removing the Japanese invaders.

May/June 1942 ~ The beginning of the end of the Japanese Empire

During the first part of the war while I was in high school, I would read in the newspapers that we were trying to establish ourselves in the South Pacific in the southern area to maintain a shipping passage for our ships to travel to and from Australia. We used Port Moresby in Papua, New Guinea as the midway point for a fuel stop, and the loss to Japan of this important port was unthinkable. To Japan, this was the next step towards the complete domination of the Pacific.

The Solomon Islands were stretched out over 800 miles and were perfect for cat and mouse warfare. Down the middle between the islands was an area 300 miles long and 60 miles wide called the slot. This was an area where some of the most ferocious naval ship to ship and man to man fighting took place in the Pacific War. The Japanese ships that roamed up and down the slot were called the Tokyo Express. You must remember this was early in the war and we were out gunned two or three ships to one. We couldn't fight them on their terms. We had to be very clever to survive. Since I wasn't there, I can only tell you I really felt for those guys. The facts speak for themselves.

Stay with me now ~ This part is pretty boring but you need to know the back ground of the action that happened prior to my getting involved personally.

August 7th 1942 ~ Guadalcanal

Admirals Turner and Fletcher brought in a strike force of 75 ships and 9,000 marines into the stinking jungle island of Guadalcanal. The two Navies fought hit and run battles that navel historians will be looking into for years.
Naval historians will study the following sea battles very carefully:

August 11th 1942 ~ Battle of Cape Esperanza

August 15th 1942 ~ Battle of Savo Island

October 25th 1942 ~ Battle of Santa Cruz

November 9th 1942 ~ Battle of Tassafaronga

November 13th 1942 ~ Battle of Guadalcanal

The Japanese losses were one carrier, two battleships, four cruisers, ten destroyers. The American losses were two carriers, seven cruisers, twenty-one destroyers, 893 planes plus 2,362 airmen and 16,000 troops. Our losses were terrific, but we turned the Tokyo Express around and sent them home saving our shipping lanes. I think we won?

April 1st 1943 ~ Go Forth and Conquer

Enough of this love making ~ I made the big decision to turn this war around and get it over with. I have just turned eighteen years old, the service is just around the corner and the world was in a mess. My football team at Belmont High (I played right end) had a perfect season score. We didn't win one game.

All of my buddies were quitting school and going into the service leaving me with no one but girls to play with (What a terrible thing). What our country was doing was no concern of mine (I thought).

But finally, Having no sense of direction, poor grades in high school, an unhappy broken home life and my exciting part-time job unloading freight trains at the Los Angeles Union Rail Station, I realized it was time to do something drastic even if it was wrong.

With a war going on and most of my friends in the service, it was the natural thing to give the service some serious consideration, so I made the big decision. I raised my right hand and joined up ~ GOODBYE, MOM AND DAD. I love you so very much but I HAVE TO GO AND WIN THE WAR! !

"Boot Camp"

San Diego

April 10th,1943

After standing around all day with about fifth naked men I
passed the army physical and I told the guy in charge that I
wanted to go into the Navy so the next thing I knew I was
on a bus trip to San Diego with all these young guys my
age. It was really fun, and my first reaction was that this
"Navy thing" was really going to be okay! Finally, we
reached the Point Loma Marine Base in San Diego. We
were assigned to a two-story barrack and I got the top
bunk bed with a small chest for my stuff. Getting
acquainted with new friends was great.

The next morning, suddenly, out of the darkness came the
blasting recording of a bugle playing something called
reveille! Then someone turned on the lights and yelled
that we had thirty minutes to dress, shave and assemble
out in front of the barracks at "Parade Rest", whatever that

39

was? Roll call was taken and off we marched for a couple of blocks to the mess hall for breakfast on metal trays. It was about this time I realized no one had asked me what I wanted to do, and it didn't look as though this was going to happen very soon either. This was a problem that was going to get a lot worse before it got better, and just maybe, I thought I had made a stupid decision along the way somewhere. I got the feeling it would be best if I were to just shut my big mouth and see what happened.

The second day, the guy in the bunk below me became very sick, so I told him I would cover for him at roll call and he should stay in this bunk until he felt better. Later that day I came back to check on him, and found him to be delirious with a heck of a fever. I reported this to the chief and they took him away to "sick bay", whatever that was! Several hours later I was asked to report to the hospital on the base. I thought I was in some kind of trouble because everyone was being real nice to me, but keeping their distance and I didn't know why. Finally, an officer asked me if I would volunteer to try and help stop an epidemic on the base. All I had to do was collect all of my friend's belongings including his bedding and every scrap of anything he might have touched and put them in a mattress

bag labeled "CONTAMINATED"! I was asked to take all of my clothes and bedding to the laundry to be washed, then get into the hottest shower I could stand and soap down at least five times, especially up my nose, eyes and in my ears. I was to get into my bunk and stay there until the next morning. Whew! I was just fine, but they took my new friend away, never to be seen again. They finally told me he had spinal meningitis, whatever that was!

Hey Boot, listen up ~

Everyone yelled at us, and stuck us with needles! They cut off all of my hair, and Issued me a new wardrobe of ill fitting uniforms and all of the necessities that would fit in a big canvas bag that was to heavy to carry but you did it anyhow. And of course, I found out about the joy of standing in line constantly. I would have complained, but no one was interested in what I thought or how I felt about anything. I learned to eat, sleep and march in step to the orders of a chief petty officer who's duty was to scream at us and counter any idea that we were a real person, and I was to do what I was told to do with no questions asked!.

They bused us out to the fields on the Marine base and we practiced shooting a rifle. Much to my surprise, I had one of the best scores in the company. Marching with our company out on the parade field with the bands playing was really great. Because of a curvature in my back bones my arms didn't want to swing the same as everyone else so they kept yelling at me to get in step and I would yell back - look at my feet, I am in step.

There was a lot of physical training but being just out of football season I was in great shape. After taking many tests it was found I had an amazing gift for any sort of skills in the area of communications, radio, signaling, whatever. So, it was no big surprise that after my "boot training" I was assigned to the Amphibious Force learning how to drive a landing craft boat. This sounded OK to me, better than sitting around listening to dots and dashes or waving flags.

06/28/1943

Landing craft school was at the submarine base in San
Diego. It amounted to riding in a large LCM landing craft
out to Coronado Island and sitting on the sand next to the
hotel in the hot sun with about a hundred other sailors
learning to signal with flags and lights, and when it was
your turn you would go aboard a landing craft and practice
driving a 36 foot craft through the waves up onto
the shore and then backing out with the waves crashing
over the stern. To do this and not lose control of your boat
was a real trick and required some real skill. I loved it, just
like body surfing at Santa Monica. No problem.

I found that I had learned all that was necessary to make a
landing in about three days and with three weeks to go, it
was time to be creative. I ran into an old school buddy who
was stationed on a submarine being repaired on the base.
When we would march down to the boat landing, we
marched by this building and I found I could step into a
doorway and spend the day with my buddy on the sub and

in a little while the crew on the sub thought I was a member of the ships company. I soon found that life on a sub is much too confining and not for me. As my company marched by later I would stand in the same doorway and step back into line. One time I had a hard time explaining why I was the only one out of a hundred men who didn't come down with food poisoning from the ham sandwiches served at lunchtime. We filled up all of the San Diego's hospitals and you had to watch where you stepped. What a mess.

I was offered the duty to stay and become an instructor for the rest of the war and be stationed in San Diego. I turned down the opportunity because there was this exciting war going on out in the Pacific and I wanted to see what it was all about. Nobody said I was very smart.

I somehow got a hold of a pass that would get me in and out of the main gate and I would hitch hike home to have dinner with mom and then go visit one of my girl friends. Then I thumbed a ride down to my old LA train station where I had worked and went in the employees' entrance and found the San Diego train. I got aboard and dismantled three seats to make a bed for sleeping on the way back on the milk train (it stopped at every town), arriving just in time for roll call in front of our barracks on base.

6-29-1943   Good bye, Dago, Hello Frisco

Finally, we were bussed to the depot and boarded a train that was so old it still had kerosene lights, and we headed for Oakland, California. It took about 15 hours to get there; sitting on side rails mostly while normal trains went by. At one of the sidings there were some "pickers" in the field and my buddy bought a bottle from one of them. We each got one of those little paper cups they have on trains and poured each of us a cup full and of course being tough sailors now, it had to be down the hatch in one swallow. It must have been tequila because I thought I was going to die from liquid fire. It felt as though my whole innards were turned inside out and I couldn't breath. (My first lesson on booze.)
Upon arriving in Oakland on the bay, there were about a

hundred of us sailors jammed onto a huge tugboat. This tug went out into the bay and down to the Alameda shipyards where we were to get our first glimpse of the big Navy fighting ship we were going to fight a war on. We went by destroyers, cruisers and aircraft carriers. This was really exciting as all of the sailors on board were yelling to the sailors aboard those beautiful ships. Finally, we went between some large ships, and there was this mangy looking ship that looked like an ugly old freighter. There were sailors aboard who were waving at us and we looked at each other and growled "Oh No" this can't be true, but sure enough this was our home and what a home it would turn out to be.

None of us "boots" had any idea as to what to expect to see and I can't say that we were really disappointed because we were already trained not to think too much and just accept what ever was dropped on us and "make do ".

06/30/1943 ~ The USS Pierce – PA50

The USS Pierce, PA50, commissioned on June 30th, 1943

was 459 feet long with a 63 foot beam, and had eight 40mms guns. We also had two 5.5" anti-aircraft guns and 30 landing craft hanging from davits on the sides of the ship. Commander A. R. Ponto was in command (an old merchant marine skipper). He was a tough looking little guy with a tiny pistol on his belt. I asked him one time about the gun and he told me he bought it for his wife to carry while he was at sea. He asked his wife what she would do if she was threatened and she said she would throw the gun at her attacker, so he gave her a rock and kept the gun for himself.

There were about a half a dozen real old (30yrs) experienced regular Navy sailors that were put on board to train us in the manly art of doing what sailors do. You were not sure whether they were human or animal but they terrorized us night and day. I learned to stay out of their way as far as possible.

07/15/1943

We finally got underway for our shakedown cruise on a cold foggy day. I remember looking straight up through the fog and seeing the bottom of the Golden Gate Bridge. The noise from the huge fog horns on each end on the bridge was beyond belief. My first duty was as a lookout up on the signal bridge. I had to continually look out with the large binoculars into the very thick fog. I couldn't see my hands in front of my face but that's Ok I was gradually learning to fallow orders.

The normal seas just outside of the bay are very large rolling waves that laid us over so far I thought we were going to capsize. I immediately got seasick. I guess it frightened the skipper too, because we turned the ship around and went back to the dock. We spent two days having cement poured into the bilges to give the ship some balace and to keep the ship from turning over. We anchored out in the bay for several days where I learned there is nowhere in the world as freezing cold and damp as San Francisco Bay in July.

July 29th 1943 ~ San Francisco

The hard hats (civilians) were still working on the ship for a couple of weeks after our arrival so we were able to go on "Liberty" into San Francisco and roam around. The women wore hats and gloves and the men were in suits and ties. Everyone was so busy. We took the cable cars up to the top of the hills and looked at this clean beautiful city. I loved it!

(What ever happened to all of those people?)

One night a few of us went to the USO where there was a band and singers on a real stage. There was a small dance floor, and the girls sat on one side and the service men on the other. We would walk across and ask a girl to dance, if and when you got up the nerve to do so. There was one young girl who was a real knockout, so I made a beeline for her. After several dances, I asked if I could see her home, She said, "Sure, Lets meet when the dance is over". Of course, all of the guys were trying to date the girls so there was an on-going discussion as to which one might be available and the order of preference. The one I had lined up was the "pick of the bunch", so I told the guys that all of the girls wanted to take me home, but I really didn't want to get involved. The guys said "Oh, Sure, that will be the day" So I said that just to be fair I will stand out in the middle of the dance floor and let some lucky girl come and get me. And they said "Oh for Sure" ~ Fortunately, my pretty little date came running out on the floor and took my hand and led me out of there. I looked back at my buddies, looked at the ceiling and shrugged.

We caught the bus, and I walked her home. She was a real sweetheart. When we got to her front door, she laid a real big passionate kiss on me, opened the door and disappeared behind the front door. I stood out on her porch in a state of shock. This was supposed to be the beginning, not the end! (Better than a poke in the eye?) So I went back to the ship in rapture. When my buddies wanted to know how she was, I said it was really too personal to talk about!

Life aboard ship was pretty rough, but when you're a kid it doesn't matter, It's kind of like "camping out". I'll talk about that later in my stories.

We got under way to San Diego Bay and it was exciting to

see the lights of MY coastal cities. I began to lose faith in our Captain when we ran into the Coronado Islands several miles south of the bay. We were too close to use radar and he didn't know which way to go. So, he turned on our spotlights to see where the rocks were. An aircraft carrier nearby radioed they would shoot our lights out, since it was navy regulations not to show any lights at night.

07/20 1943

The next morning we anchored in the bay and our boat crews were taken to the Higgins boat yard to pick up the boats for our ship. Our ship had 30 wooden LCVP's boats and two CPM iron tank boats. On the way back to our ship one of the boats started to sink, so I lashed it securely to my boat with several lines and managed to get the sinking boat back to our ship. I was the hero of the day. I learned later that, that's not a very smart thing to do. The ship had what they called "davits" with hooks that we connected to our boat and we were lifted up to the deck and secured to the ship. I now had a real fighting craft that

Had two 20 millimeter machineguns on the stern (back) that was all mine. I'm ready to go to war.

07/23/1943

From San Diego we headed out to sea and the Hawaii Islands.

"YO, HO, HO and a Bottle of Rum!" I'm a real sailor now. ~ Look out Japos ~ here I come . . . . Arrrgggh

After days of nothing but water for 360 degrees and after our fiasco in San Diego, I wasn't at all sure we would ever see land again. On the third or forth day it does sort of get to you to wake up every morning wlth the ship plowing through the water and see nothing but water as far as far as you can see in all directions. You swear that you are going around in circles.

Christopher Columbus must have been a real nut. A real cheer went up on the fifth day when Diamond Head appeared on the horizon. Dirt never looked so good.

07/25/1943 ~ The Sea Story I Didn't Tell Mom About

Arriving in Pearl Harbor, I was really astounded to see that
after a year and a half our battle wagons were still resting
on their sides and all the buildings riddled with bullet
holes. You think, hey, these guys were not kidding around!
This is serious stuff going on here. Your insides churn and
you suddenly have a fierce and personal determination to
take whatever effort necessary to make someone pay for
this horrible sight. To know that these ships are STILL
FULL OF SAILORS, JUST LIKE ME. (IS THIS GOING TO
HAPPEN TO MY SHIP?) A person could really get them
self killed or something. And that was very frightening to
say the least!
I was excited about being a real sailor out in the middle of
the ocean, and could not wait to go ashore to see the
natives in this tropical paradise. I put on my new "whites"
and since it was raining, a new raincoat. Then with a
couple of buddies we caught the bus for downtown
Honolulu. It was a crummy little harbor town full of sailors

just like me, and not a native to be found anywhere. The first thing that happened was I noticed everyone looking at me and smiling. I finally asked one of my buddies what was going on, and he said only an idiot would wear a hot raincoat in the tropics! I was so embarrassed. I took it off and stuffed it in a trash barrel. Everywhere you looked the scenery was so beautiful but when you finished that you looked around for something to do. There were lots of crummy little bars but they were reserved for those that like to get drunk and fight but I didn't know how to do that.

Does anyone have ten dollars ?

The Admirals (my) boat and the 2nd division crew

Liberty at the Royal Hawaiian

I was hungry and I noticed a long line of sailors waiting to go into a certain building. So I figured it must be a good place to eat, and we got in line. My buddies told me that we could eat later. This line was for satisfying one's sexual desires (that's not exactly the way they put it) and I said "forget it"! But they said, "THIS IS WHAT SAILORS DO", so what can a sailor do?. I had to go along with them, right? As I stood in line, I kept thinking about those pictures that were shown to us in boot camp of guys rotting away with venereal diseases. So by the time I got to the head of the line, I was paranoid. I told the lady I didn't think I was ready for this and she said, "Okay Boot", you can sit over there and wait for your friends". As I sat and watched, I noticed there were several naked women running from room to room. ~ Wow - is that what they look like ?. One room was for a sailor to remove his clothes and where the lady did her work, I was told that the sailors were so excited that when the lady put her hand on them and it was all over. In a few minutes she would move to the next room and the sailor would be replaced. Henry Ford would have been proud of these gals, as this was a really smooth running assembly line. I was told the Navy supplied these women and gave them weekly examinations. If I had known at the time that I WOULDENT see another white woman for the next two and a half years, I think I would have given this whole thing some serious consideration.

Later on as we walked down the street, I noticed another line, but this time it was for having your picture taken with a native girl in a skimpy little outfit made of tie leaves. The photographer would place the girl in front of the sailor with his arms around her and snap the picture. While I was giving this some serious thought, I noticed that the same guys were going through the line again. This seemed strange so I looked a little closer and noticed that just as the picture was snapped, the girl would reach down around behind her back and grab the sailor! The expressions on their faces in those pictures were priceless!

We caught a taxi and for 7.50 each we went out through sugar cane and pineapple fields for about an hour arriving at Waikiki Beach. There were two hotels, Can you believe that?. One was the Moauna and the other was the

Pink Royal Hawaiian. They were the most beautiful hotels that I had ever seen. They were used for housing the sailors from submarines when they were in port (such a deal)! These guys really did deserve all of the benefits possible. There were a few bars and food stands along the road. There was no whiskey on the island, but you could buy as many rum and cokes as you wanted and sit under the world's largest Banyan Tree at the Moauna hotel. Once a day they would have some hula dancing girls performed for us. The beach had little or no sand (just coral) with a gated barbed wire fence running along the waters edge. You could buy a bathing suit, rent a locker, surfboard and go swimming. I found standing up on a surfboard (and they were just old boards) in the waves was impossible as well as dangerous due to the coral reefs.

The father of one of my girl friends in Hollywood managed a small hospital there. It was nice to visit him for lunch and to see real, honest to God people. I found that the people who lived there permanently never went to the shoreline because of the hoards of sailors. They lived a very quiet, low-key lifestyle and enjoyed their paradise up on the mountainsides far inland.

09/01/1943 ~ Drinking the hard Stuff

A Chinese photographer in Honolulu took the picture of me in the front of this little book. I had to have pictures for my folks and girl friends back home so they wouldn't forget me. When my friends saw the pictures, they all went to this guy and had their picture taken also Several days later I stopped in to see him and he had a fifth of bourbon for me
as a gift for all the business I brought him. We knew it was against the law to bring hard liquor on a ship so we found a shoe box to put it in and wrapped it with a whole lot of heavy string to make it difficult to get into. I put on my innocent face and with a large shopping bag, the marines at the gate didn't give me a second look.

A couple of weeks later out at sea I was sitting around in my boat with my crummy friends and they were moaning about how long it had been since they had a decent drink of whiskey. Of course being a big shot that I was I casually mentioned that I had a bottle I was saving to celebrate the end of the war. I got the reaction I expected. They said they would break my arm if I didn't produce the bottle.

We passed the bottle around and took sips until it was gone. They thought they were in heaven, but I got so sick I passed out and threw up all over my boat. Other than on that train, this was my first experience with the awful stuff.

During the first part of my Pacific tour, I was in and out of the Hawaiian Islands many times. I learned to love them all and vowed to return some day, which of course; I have done many times.

In the Philippines during the invasion I bought a couple of bottles for ten bucks of what they promised were their best stuff. They were in long thin bottles that looked really exciting. I took them back to the ship and sold them for forty dollars each. This one guy from the hills of Virginia drank just what was in the neck of the bottle and he didn't move for two days with his eyes wide open. I kept checking to see if he was breathing. I thought I had killed him.

I went to the guy who bought the other bottle and tried to buy it back, but he had raffled it off for a dollar per chance and sold a hundred chances, and said he didn't know who won. I told him he was most likely committing murder and he had better find that bottle and throw it over the side. I sweated bullets over this adventure, but nothing ever came of it. I gave the booze one more try in Manila while waiting for a ship to take me home. I ended up spending the night in a drainage ditch along side of the road on my way back to the base. I didn't need any more lessons. That WAS IT.

10/01/1943 ~ Maui, Hawaii

While making practice landings with the Marines on
The beautiful sands of (no coral) Kaanapoli Beach in Maui,
There were times when the troops were ashore playing war games. So, I would slip away and cruise up or down the coast to do a little sightseeing on my own. It was against the rules but with me timing was everything. I went by

some of the most beautiful bays I had ever seen and promised myself I would return to this heavenly place. As it turned out, I have spent many family vacations at my favorite spot, The Napili Bay Beach Club in Maui, But I'm getting ahead of my story.

There were huge waves crashing on the beach, so being a "Super California Surfer", I had to give these big rollers a try, I suddenly ran into something I had never seen before. There were coral reefs sticking out of the water like knives. As I was pounded into them, I thought I would never get out alive, but I did make it back to the boat. I was ripped open from head to toe! I laid down on the stern and my deck hand poured iodine all over me. What a mess! I soon learned that the juice of a lime will stop coral infection.
I ave since snorkeled the area many times and have made friends with a couple of big Groupers (I swear they are the same ones), but I never lost my respect for the beautiful (but dangerous) coral reefs.

Days later I landed my boat on the same beach to look for coconuts. They were all over the ground. So I gathered up an armload and started back to the boat when a lovely native girl came out from behind the trees asking me to stop. I didn't know if I was in trouble, but I sure liked what I saw. She proceeded to show me how to choose the ripe coconuts from the bad. I was about to ask her to go for a ride in my boat when this big "Wahine" guy showed up. He was very nice, but it was very obvious it was time for me to go! I thanked her very much and went back to the boat with all of my "good coconuts".

A month or so later on the beach at Makin Island during the bloody landings, I went looking for good fresh coconuts. I finally found about a half dozen and started to go back to the beach when all hell broke loose! All of the troops standing around dropped to the ground and started shooting their guns up into the air. I yelled at a soldier asking what in the world was happening, and he pointed up and yelled that a Jap was hiding up in the trees over our heads and shooting soldiers through the top of their heads.

You can imagine the sudden terror of a stupid sailor standing there! Coconuts went flying in the air and my feet didn't hit the ground until I was safely back in my boat! The guys in the boat wanted to know where were the coconuts?. So I made it very clear what they could do with any coconuts lying around.

Our ship was assigned to the Fifth Amphibious Force and sent to the Island of Maui for two weeks of intensive training in amphibious and gunnery warfare. For me this meant my boat would be lowered into the water with 36 Army or Marine troops, and I would go to an assigned circle of boats. Then on a signal we would head for the beach and finally make a wave parallel to the shore. From there we would maneuver our way though the surf and up onto the sand. I would drop the bow ramp with the troops then running out onto the beach. We would then raise the ramp and back away from the beach and return to the ship for another load of troops. The big shot Marines and the Navy never really got along in town. So just for fun, I would go a little bit faster and hit the waves on a slight angle and by the time we got to the beach, all of the troops were soaking wet and so seasick they could hardly stand up. The Army was okay. This went on for hours and hours everyday. We had to do something to pass the time of day. During this training period I was chosen to help with an experiment that was interesting. One day an officer brought down to my boat long thin shells and racks to hold them on an angle. We went to an island the Navy used for aircraft bombing practice. He loaded the racks with the rockets, six on each side. As we reached about a hundred feet from shore he pressed a switch, and the rockets exploded. They went whistling into the shore area and exploded on contact with the beach. The officer said the rockets would kill anything within twenty-five feet. We proceeded to make several runs onto the beach firing one, two and three at a time. The problem was he would fire at the wrong moment with the boat going up and down and the rockets went all over the place. If he had let me fire them I would have worked out the right timing to fire. It's very common now to see many racks on the decks of LSTs shooting hundreds of rockets in to the shoreline. "But I was the first?"

As far as my general duties were concerned, life aboard ship was very boring and repetitious except when about 700 men (boys 18 to 35) were jammed into such a small area, there was built-in chaos 24 hours a day. As for work, the deck hands cleaned and painted. The boat crews maintained our boats in perfect condition at all times. I found that it was easer to paint the boat than cleaning it. On an iron ship sitting on salt water in the sun and rain with 24 hours a day of humidity, there is one constant problem, And that is RUST? It was everywhere. The deck crew started at the bow and roped off an area, chipped off all of the rust and paint, painted the deck with two coats of rust preservation and two coats of navy gray paint. Then the crew moved back about thirty feet and started all over again. This was done over and over until they were at the stern and every square inch of the ship was painted. Then they moved to the bow and started over again. The crew had to move fast to stay ahead of the rust.

The ship's company are made up of many diverse divisions of men trained to do a particular job or duty. There were cooks, boiler makers, bookkeepers and garbage grinders. We had a great number of communication and radar people, about a hundred boat operators and about a hundred deck sailors. The cooks served liver and onions once a week. On that day I ate peanut butter and jelly sandwiches, considering the conditions the food was really pretty good. Because of the volume of food prepared everyday they didn't worry about how good it tasted   We spent part of our time picking weevils out of the bead. We had a machine about as big as a cow that mixed powder and water for milk and no fresh vegetables accept when we were in port.

My body started to rebel and I broke out with "weeping China crud" especially under my arms, crotch and feet. I was exhausted all of the time. The medics had a white cream that felt good and they rubbed it all over you. I would then go up to my boat and lie down. About that time it felt as though I was on fire for about an hour. The medics also had a solution they poured all over you, and wherever there was an open sore it would turn a bright purple. The sore dried hard. You can imagine how sad we looked. We just smiled and carried on. We called it "Asiatic conditioning".

I soon got used to the system and lifestyle, but I didn't like the discipline. I had a good sense of humor and kept everyone around me laughing. The life style was better than what I had left behind at home.

I really enjoyed my boat, and I thought I was the best coxswain in the Navy. Any boat going in the same direction as I was heading I challenged to a race (One thing I didn't like was a nasty rumor that only a few of us coxswains would be returning home, "EVER". In order to see where I was going I had to stand up tall to see over the ramp at the bow and I made a great target.)

I slept in a room (compartment) about 30' X 60' with about 100 guys on hanging wire shelves about five high. We had a four-inch mattress, a sheet and a light blanket. When you were in your bunk there was about a foot between you and the bed above you, that was it. There was no air-conditioning, just a fan that blew in hot air. We each had a normal gym locker for our stuff. There were "heads" designed for a bunch of pigs. As soon as we reached warm weather, I slept topside in my boat that hung over the side of the ship. I used a life saving ring and a bucket full of water for a toilet. (How's that for a visual description?).

The diversity of the crew was really an education in it's self. They were from the hills of Virginia, the tip of Florida, Pennsylvania coal miners, New Youakers, Arkies, Oakies and lots of farm boys. They loved to talk about how high the snow would pile up and freeze and the floods in the spring. I asked if they were going to go back there and they said "Of course, that's where I live" and I would say -Why? I found a picture in a magazine with an orange grove with lots of oranges and a mountain covered with snow in the back ground. I said "We only play in the snow on week ends." There were only a few "normal city boys" like me. Being from the Hollywood area meant you were very rich and very queer, of course I was neither. We were special people because we Thought so. I remember one kid telling me how tough it was at home and I said, "I know". He said "How would a rich guy like you know anything?" I just laughed. If only he knew. The kids from up in the hills all played guitars and they drove me crazy. They loved to play all of the old songs, but they played one song and sang the words from another at the same time. If a person tried to correct them, they would offer to break your arm.

I will say the following just once so that I don't bore you to much but it was a daily happening and never to be forgotten. At sea, the rolling and wistful clouds with the golden setting sun and especially the sunrise peeking over the horizon or the huge bright full moon making a road of silver on a calm sea is like magic and of course the Unbelievable huge crashing waves with shrieking winds in a storm are so exciting. It's hard to believe that one can get used to the floor (deck) moving in all directions and hardly give it a thought. While eating you held on to your tray with one hand. Where I came from, earth quakes happened on a regular basis so this was no big deal. One thing that was kind of nice was that there was no dirt or dust as everything was cleaned everyday until there was no dirt at all. Sharing this with hundreds of sailors is not the same by any measure as being with a girl you love .on a cruise ship

I can't remember why but one day our ship went around to the other side of the island to it's little sea port of Kahalua I remember walking down the main street about two city blocks long and buying some fruit from a real native Hawaiian. They were very quite smiling folks with copper skins and long black hair. I was fascinated with there low key way of life. It didn't' seem to matter where you looked the view was unbelievably beautiful. The warm winds, lush green mountains, the clear blue sky and the soft blue green waters. Many years later when my son finished college and wanted to go there and start a new business called "Maui Sunburst" to raise tropical flowers and sell them all over the world. I said "go for it" with a great deal of envy. You know the old saying " If I had known he was going to be rich I would have been nicer to him as a child."

Japanese Admiral Yamamoto

Admiral Yamamoto was the genius behind the attack on

Pearl Harbor and the number one Japanese planner for the Navy. He was on an inspection tour of the southern most islands. Our number one decrypting genius Joseph Rochefors and staff were able to decode a message indicating that the Admiral would be flying into their huge Truck Island Naval Base. Our Admiral Kincade dispatched a squadron of P-38s and they caught up with him as he was going in for a landing and blew him out of the sky. This was a tremendous blow to Japans future.

The Gilbert Island Atoll

Makin Island Atoll

Tarawa Island Atoll

11/15/1943 The Invasion of the Gilbert Atoll

After three of four weeks training at Maui we went back to
Pearl Harbor for the loading of supplies, ammunition and a
full ship load of Army personnel. We were ready to cast off
for a major experience in our young lives. If there was ever
a feeling of apprehension in the air, it was now. We were
venturing out into the waters controlled by Japanese
submarines and aircraft, and finally we were on the

74

offensive rather than the defensive. All I could think of was those ships lying on the bottom at Pearl Harbor.   It's rather disconcerting to know that you might be blown out of the water at any moment and this was no joke, this was real, Our ships were being blown out of the water all over the Pacific at that very minute.

We were in two lines of many transports and many cargo vessels surrounded by cruisers, destroyers and a couple of carriers. There were ships as far as the eye could see in all directions. Our decks were covered with soldiers who were playing cards, cleaning their guns or sharpening their knives. Every once in a while, one of them would fall over board, and of course, we couldn't stop. We were told that there was a minesweeper following behind the fleet to pick them up.

We set our course for Tarawa (Butaritari) and Makin (Betio) Islands in the Gilbert Atoll (the first islands with airstrips) and we were ready to avenge Pearl Harbor. As a landing craft coxswain, you are not part of the deck crew so they find duty that is out of the ordinary for you. For some reason, I was chosen to become a helmsman. That means you stand watch at the wheel up on the bridge with the captain and the officers on deck duties. There's a lot of pressure that goes along with this job. You stand for two hours with eyes glued to a large compass, turning the wheel port and starboard as many degrees as ordered by the officer of the deck who is following the orders of our navigator. You are following a submarine coarse witch means that you are constantly moving like a snake so that you never give a submarine a straight shot with a torpedo. There are no margins for error as all of the "Stars and Bars" are looking down your neck. After two hours your eyes fog up, so you trade places with another helmsman that is down on the stern of the ship over the rudder where another wheel and compass are located. Earphones at this station connect you to the next in command officer just in case some lucky Japanese plane blows the bridge away. . It's a real trick keeping all of the ships in formation from running into each other because of the wind and tide forces. The course changes require the helmsman to constantly spin the wheel to stay on the proper degree and course. While standing at the wheel, you can look out of a port hole at the bow of the ship as it plows through the sea ahead of you. This can be very exciting in high seas. I soon learned that as the bow would rise and fall, the ship would move to the right or left depending on the tides and winds throwing you off course. Most people don't realize that the sides of a ship (from the deck to the sea) are like giant sails with the winds pushing you constantly. So the Officer of the Deck is calling out a new compass headings bringing you back on course every few minutes.

I found that when the bow went up and down for the second time, I could move the compass heading a couple of degrees and stay on the ship's original course. I had to be very careful not to let anyone see me do this as we were not supposed to think, but just to "follow orders". The fun part was when I was at the helm; we were always on course. This drove the Officer of the Deck crazy! Both he and the Captain said it had to be me, but they couldn't figure out what I was doing, and of course, I put on my most innocent face.

The other thing I did that drove everybody nuts was, I

found I had very unusual night vision. When we were following another ship without any lights on in the bridge, the officer with his binoculars watching the ship ahead would call out a compass bearing. Of course I could see the ship and keep moving the wheel just slightly to stay in line. The Captain would slip around behind me in the dark trying to find out what I was doing, but he had a sinus problem and I could hear him breathing! I know I was quite a topic of conversation in the officers quarters.

One time on watch, I was fascinated by the fact I could see a destroyer out of one of the side portholes and it was firing its five-inch shells at a practice target. When I looked back at the ship we were following, it was gone! I finally spotted it and gave full rudder to bring us back in position. When the Captain realized what was happening he yelled and came running up to me, wanting to know what the hell I was doing! He stared at me for about five seconds and said, "I'll bet you never do that again!" And I said "no-o-o-o sir! He then walked back to his chair on the starboard side of the bridge shaking his head! It's amazing how creative you can be when you're bored to tears. Our

Captain was a very colorful, old (about 50) merchant marine skipper before the war. So, he was not the normal "spit and polish" officer. When we would enter or leave port he would take over the bridge and it was an experience to listen to him say "Take her over this away a little, now take her back to the port a little" and so on. One time I asked how far was "a little". He gave me a dumb look and said "Son, if you can't figure that out you don't belong on this bridge!" To be a qualified helmsman and one of the few people in the world to know the feeling of having a huge ship respond to your touch while crashing through the waves is a thrill you'll never forget! Once you are "one with the sea", you are a sailor forever and ever.

Finally, at dawn one morning we reached our target, Makin Island in the Gilbert Atoll, and it certainly did not look very

imposing. It was a pretty little sand strip with palm trees. I
said "Hell, I can do this all by myself"!

11/20/1943

Everything was extremely quiet. If a guy was ever going to
say his prayers this was it. There were priests aboard that
were praying for the troops We were ready to do what we
had come to do. Then suddenly we heard over the loud
speakers a shrill of the boatswains pipe and he yelled
"AWAY ALL BOATS ~ AWAY ALL BOATS", and down we
went into the water where the 165th Infantry Regiment of
the 27th division started climbing down the nets on the
sides of the ship into our boats. One of the first men into
my boat was a guy about 6' x 6". He was about three
hundred pounds with hand grenades hanging all down the
front of his chest, a large machine gun and his face was
painted black and green to match his uniform. I thought to
myself that if we sent him in first, the rest of us could go
home. He would scare all those little Jap's to death!
When I had my boat loaded with 36 men, I joined my
predetermined position with the other boats circling around

waiting for the signal to head for the shore. Finally the signal "Roger" went up. We formed our parallel lines and took off for the beach. Well, what do you know ?. I'm in the first wave to hit the beach. This didn't seem to be what I had in mind when I joined this mans Navy, but nobody said life was fair. But you truly didn't have time to think, and you just kept your eyes on the shore. When we were about a city block from the beach, I heard this loud roar and darned if a F4F Navy Wildcat aircraft didn't just pancake in for a landing right beside my boat. It just sat there for a moment. Then the pilot opened the overhead canopy and stood up, blew up his May West life jacket and the plane went right down, leaving the pilot floating in the water. I started to go over and pick him up, but another boat got to him first and we all continued on toward the island.

I'll bet he was the only Navy pilot that was strafing the beach, was shot down and made an assault landing straight into the same machine gun fire that shot him down just a few minutes before, all in the same morning. I hope he lived to tell the story.

We finally got the signal (pumping our right fist and arm up and down) that we were on our own. It was full speed ahead and with the boat sitting low the salt water was flying over the sides of the boat into my face burning my eyes. Suddenly the realization struck home that this was no practice run. This was the real thing! I looked down into my boat and there were thirty-six soldier boys looking up at me, and nobody is smiling. Just an expression of cold fear and determination. It was then I realized that until I ran my boat up on the beach and we dropped our bow ramp I was personally responsible for each of their lives. I remember well how my heart started pounding in my chest as the shells coming from the shore started hitting water around us. The soldiers got down on their knees, trying to get lower than the water lIne of the boat. Some of them couldn't stand not knowing what was happening and got up on their feet to peek over the side railing. I screamed at them, yelling "Get down or die"

About a hundred feet from shore I slammed into a coral
reef. I backed up and headed off in a different direction

bouncing off of more reefs, and trying to find my way

between the jagged peaks just below the water line. I was
still too far from the sand to stop, so it was back and forth

over and around coral and rocks. I just had to get these troops close enough for them to stand up in the surf. Once they were in the water and on their feet it was up to them to do what they came to do.

The shore became a wall of flames as our aircraft strafed and bombed the beach, while the ships behind us were bombarding the shoreline with their big guns and rockets! The huge shells were screaming in just a few feet over our heads. As we got closer to shore, I was fascinated by some of the shells that didn't explode when they hit the beach. They just skipped into the coconut trees causing them to fly in all directions. The screaming of the shells and the concussion of the explosions is truly indescribable!

About this time, my deck hand Sanchez and my motor machinist Smith, started firing their 20-millimeter machine guns mounted on the stern of our boat. The shells from one of the guns was whistling so close to my head, I yelled at Smith to stop firing, but he said his gun turret was stuck and it wouldn't swivel. He was not about to stop firing, This was his war too. I asked a soldier to hold my steering wheel while I jumped up on the stern. You know what they say about your strength in the heat of battle, I picked up the heavy turret and shook it loose and set it right down on my big toe. The gun worked fine but I was the first casualty of the invasion! (Boy, did it hurt!)

When I looked for a place to land my boat, I saw a large gun emplacement with the long barrel pointed directly at me. I figured they were waiting for me to drop the ramp on the front of the boat and then blow us out of the water for sure, but there was no time to worry about that. The Japanese machine guns were different than ours, they made a funny popping sound like a kid's toy and the water around us looked as though it was raining. The large ramp at the bow was heavy metal and there was a sheet of metal down the sides of the boat. When the Jap shells hit them it made a sound you will not soon forget.

 My common sense said to drop down in the bottom of the boat but who would operate the boat?. I realized what they meant when they said that most boat coxswains were "on a one way trip"! I felt like I was in a trance, my heart was pounding so hard and I felt like throwing up but you do what you are trained to do because there is nothing to else to do.

About fifty feet from the beach I realized I could go no further as the reef was like a wall just below the surface. I yelled at Sanchez to drop the ramp and screamed at the troops to get the hell out of my boat and "God Bless You All!" They were down on their knees trying not to get hit by machine gun fire, but they jumped up and went dashing out into about three to five feet of water (the coral was full of large holes). I have no idea if any of them made it to shore. You will read a lot about the brave Japanese Kamikaze pilots that dived into our ships, but I can tell you that no one could be more brave than those Army soldiers and Marines who were in the first waves to hit the beach!

We rolled up the ramp and without the weight of the troops, we were high in the water and able to get over the coral and out of there fast. It was about then I remembered that big gun emplacement and thanked the

Lord for small things.

But then, it was back to the ship for another load of troops.
On the way back I found a great big soldier spread eagle
on the deck of my boat. He was so sea sick he had
heaved all over himself and was so weak he couldn't
move. When we got to the ship, they had to lower a
stretcher attached to a boom line to lift him back aboard.
Once again we loaded up with troops. As we approached
the shoreline again, we were slapped in the face with the
smell of death   The odor of decomposing bodies and
those killed with flame throwers is something you will never
forget! as long as you live and they were all over the place.
The troops had established a beachhead and I could make
it all the way to the sand this time. As the troops hit the
beach we were able to run out on the beach and pick up
many of the wounded off the sand and carry them into our
boat. We had a large box of sulfanilamide powder to pour
on their wounds. The screaming ones were not as badly
hurt as the quiet ones. They were all in shock from terrible
wounds. Some required a shot of morphine. (We drew a
large "M" on their foreheads with their own blood so the

doctors aboard ship would know not to give these men more morphine.)

One thing that was buried in the back of my mind was remembering the time that I was holding the head of my little niece (Judy) like a football while the doctor sewed up a two inch cut on her head. There was a lot of blood and when he was finished I passed out. I really worried about that happening again but I was so involved I didn't think of until the invasion was over.

The water and salt spray would dry white on your eyebrows and when you cried your eyes burned so much you couldn't see where you were going. (It was ok to cry) After many trips back and forth to the beach with supplies and ammunition, things slowed down a little. So I checked out that gun emplacement on shore that had frightened me, only to find it was a section of a trunk of a palm tree sticking out of a pile of sand bags, (dirty birds!).

By now my big toe was a blue green monster and I had the time to do some hurting on my own, but for some reason no one felt very sorry for me. While my boat was being loaded, I made a quick trip to our sick bay to see if a doctor could help me. When I arrived, there were two doctors on each side of the operating table. The men would be brought in on a stretcher and set down on the table. Then the doctors dived in, cutting the bullets and shrapnel out and sewing the guy up. There were about twenty stretchers waiting in line on the deck. Someone wanted to know if they could help me and I said, "No thanks, I'm just fine!" So, I just whimpered a lot about not getting a Purple Heart or a Congressional Medal of Honor for all the suffering my big toe caused.

As the sun went down, the ships went out to sea so they wouldn't be sitting targets for the submarines, so we tied our boats together and made a little island just out of range of the guns on shore. We were exhausted, but couldn't sleep because of the sounds of the men on shore trying to kill each other. We thanked God we were in the Navy. I said over and over "This is all wrong!" War is Hell.

We started at one end of the island and slowly moved from one end to the other. When our troops reached the other end there were several Japanese soldiers that made their way out onto the coral reef that was about a city block from shore. They just sat out there in the water. I had heard that Japanese would not give up because they were told that we were cruel and inhuman and would touchier them.

Just as I was trying to think of a way to take my boat out there and pick them up, three of our troops sat down on the sand and with their guns and killed off the Jap's one by one. How about that, they were right, we were cruel and inhuman. Later on I saw a couple guys with a necklace strung with gold teeth. This really bothered me and I found it very difficult to understand. I guess that when you have watched your buddies on all sides of you get blown away, You just become a different kind of a person. When I saw our troops dig a trench with a bulldozer to create a mass grave for the enemy it reminded me of pictures of the Germans doing the same thing. ~ War is Hell

You may wonder about our food, it may not mean much to you in the heat of battle but to an eighteen years old, a war, death and destruction comes in second to being hungry. When we were unloading supplies on the beach for the troops, if a case of rations looked interesting it would end up back between our fuel tanks. One case happened to be canned pineapple, boy were they good. I finished off a couple of cans and soon became violently sick. It was at least twenty years before I would taste them again. Our K-rations came in small cans (Scrambled eggs, spam and beans/rice) we lined them up on the engine manifold so they were always hot and ready to eat. They weren't all that bad with coconut milk.

Someone yelled and we looked at a huge fireball on the horizon. Something in my stomach went clunk. The aircraft carrier, Liscomb Ray, caught a torpedo and almost everyone on the ship was lost! Each of us imagined it was our own ship, so we were thrilled to see the ship with PA50 on its bow come over the horizon! Then it was back to war we go.

Our beach masters blew up the coral reefs so we could

make it to the sand and unload. There were flags for troops, ammunition, food, tanks, jeeps so you knew where to land your cargo. The action was something to watch, everyone was moving as fast as you can go trying to unload your stuff and fill your deck with the wounded.

Then it we full speed ahead back to your ship.
I've always said that if you didn't get killed, it was just another experience to remember. It's no big deal. Life is full of unhappiness, so carry on. The other night I went to see the film "Saving Privet Ryan" and was prepared to see another old war movie. As the picture began and the sounds began to rumble, I started to tremble. As I heard the shells fly over head, I began to shake and as the bullets tore into the troops, I started crying! I completely lost all control, and I'm shaking right now as I write this. It was several days before I could discuss it with my wife. I had no idea I had been carrying all this pain around inside me for over 60 years.
Admiral Spruance was the overall Commander with Admiral Turner in charge of the amphibious landings and Marine General Halland Smith was in charge of the troops.

We hit the beach with tragic miscalculation of the tides. It's hard to believe such a thing could happen In those early days there was a whole lot about the ocean that we didn't know but you would think they would have known not to send us in over the coral reefs at low tide. The battle for the Makin, and Tarawa Islands lasted only three days, but we lost over 1,080 lives and 2,292 wounded! The Japanese lost over 4,000 lives with no wounded. The islands were secured on February 7th1944.

On our way to the invasion our ship was jammed with soldiers boys and enjoying their first cruise on the high seas. We were ready and determined to fight the world for our country. When the invasion was over each one of us had little or nothing to say to each other. We were alive and didn't know why. We had just lived through one of the most horrible experiences know to man. We just stared out to sea in a state of shock. You were well aware of the fact that you were no longer a boy, you are now a hardened warrior and contrary to what we expected this was not a good feeling at all and you were going to have to live with it the rest of your our life. ~ War is Hell

The look of a man that was a boy a few hours ago

(OK Milt) You just participated in the successful effort to kill 4,000 human beings. You didn't know any of these people, and they didn't know you. Why did you kill them? Why did they try to kill you? How can we make any sense out of this? Obviously, taking away their oil was not a very nice thing to do, and left them with the only one choice. That was capturing the oil fields in South East Asia, and starting a war with us. It seems logical that President Roosevelt could have sat down with Tojo or somebody and worked out a compromise on the oil situation. Was there no opportunity to work out something? The world is full of oil! The Japanese soldiers were a formidable force to deal with. Why? As an example, a little Japanese guy was sent to this little island in the middle of the Pacific and told NOT to wave a white flag when completely surrounded. He was to sit there in a hole in the ground and kill as many of us as he could until he was blown to pieces! If he was not killed then he was to commit seppuku, (suicide.) And he did it. Why? I'm told to do a lot of things I don't do. Remember the little Japanese boy who tried to take my ball at school? I almost accidentally killed him. He could have been that Japanese soldier in the in the hole in the ground on that particular island. OK, so I have to defend my wonderful country, or I have to agree that someone has to do what our President decided we should do. I still get the feeling there is something terribly wrong here. But all right, I love my country - I will follow orders – most of the time.

One Tough Dude

On one of the trips back and forth from ship to shore, I had one little mishap that makes me smile when I remember it. The waves were rising and falling four or five feet high when I pulled along side the ship, the crew was ready to lower a jeep into my boat. In this process, the timing is everything. When I maneuvered my boat to just the right spot and signaled them to drop the jeep, nothing happened. A couple of seconds later, of course the boat moved, and they dropped the jeep on top of me. I fell to the deck and the jeep smashed the engine cover and bent my steering wheel. Fortunately, it didn't drop quite low enough to flatten me, but it was close!

They lifted the jeep off of me, and I was so highly emotional that I yelled at my deck hand to take the wheel and proceeded to climb up the rope netting on the side of the ship. When I reached the railing I screamed at the man in charge of the winch, telling him that he was a stupid "so and so and so and so", and he was to take his orders from me and NO one else! I managed to climb back down to the boat and then timed the waves to drop the jeep properly.

My deck hand laughed and said. "Do you have any idea who you were talking to?" He said that it was the ship's Chief Warrant officer. This officer starts out as an enlisted man and works his way up to being the old pro that knows everything and is in charge of everything that happened in the operations of the ship's deck crew. (One of the most feared and respected men on the ship, I might add.) He had a rope tattoo around his wrists and neck. The rest of his body was covered with old pictures from his China Seas duty. A couple of his front teeth were knocked out and replaced with gold ones! This was one tough dude that never smiled at anyone! Later, on the way back to

Pearl Harbor, I met him face to face in a passageway. He reached over and grabbed me by the shirt and pulled me up close to his face. He said, "listen up! No one talks to me the way you did and lives". He said the only thing that saved my butt was that I was absolutely correct and he wanted to apologize to me for his mistake. As soon as I was able to talk, I told him that I was honored to accept his apology, and I'm sure this had never happed before, and would never happen again! We both laughed and went on our merry way.

All of the elements of suffering was in their eyes. On one of my trips to shore with supplies I noticed an Army officer waiting for my boat to be unloaded. He then entered the boat and said that he wanted to commandeer my boat for a "Special Problem", so I said, "Sounds good to me, let's go!" We went along the shore for a few minutes and then he told me to go in for a landing. I told him that there were bad guys in there who didn't like me. He said, "Let's go anyhow. You'll be really glad you did, that's IF you don't get killed." I said, "won-der-ful!" and in we went. When we made it through the coral and hit the sand, we lowered the front ramp and he ran out into the trees and bushes. I sat there like a fool waiting for the Japs to blast us away. A few minutes later a whole bunch of Polynesian people (30 to 40) came out and hurried down into my boat. Once they were all jammed in we rolled up the ramp and backed out of there.

When I asked. "Now what?" he said to head out across the lagoon to any little island they wanted to go to. He talked to some of the older men (I mean really old) and they pointed out an island about a mile or two away that was about a city block square. The women and girls, who were in old tattered and torn house dresses, They had bronzed color skin with long flowing black hair. The younger girls were quite lovely, they sat down on the deck and the men and boys in cut off pants held on to the sides of the boat. There was no crying or hysteria, just blank stares looking up at me. I couldn't help but wonder how these sweet and innocent people could have survived all of the tremendous bombing and strafing from our aircraft in the last few weeks. They must have lost many of their family members they had to be below the surface of the ground to have survived. I'm sure they had no idea what was happening to them. They understood English, but had nothing to say. Their faces with wide eyes seemed to say, "Please take me somewhere that's safe, please!"

After unloading them on the sand, I pulled away knowing I would never, ever forget looking back at this little group of people standing together so closely, and waving very slowly. I didn't know whether they were sad or happy, but I knew they were safe and that gave me a warm feeling down inside. The Army officer said he would see that they would be supplied food and water.

The kicker to this little story is that when my wife and I went on a Hawaiian cruise recently, one of the islands on the tour was Fanning Island in the Gilbert Island Lagoon. While walking around, I had this strange feeling of "déjà vu" down inside. There was a little old man sitting at a make shift table selling small pieces of reef coral that were quite pretty, so I bought a piece to add to my collection at home. I asked him if he was here sixty years ago. He gave me a strange look and nodded "yes". I said, "So was

I!" He jumped up and ran around the table, grabbing my hand in both of his, and without saying anything he just looked up at me with that same look I remembered in the eyes of those sweet people standing in my boat so long, long ago! I'm telling you, it was spooky. If I could do it over again, I would have bought his whole stock of coral, even though I could have walked about twenty feet and picked up all I wanted off the beach. I guess I was just in a state of shock.

11/20/1943 ~ A Little Humor

Always looking for a way to make a buck, I found that the crews on the ships were sitting there looking at the island and all of the action except our boat crews were the only ones who had access to the smoking beach and the muck and mire. So they would pay big bucks for any kind of souvenir that they could send or take to the folks back home. So I was constantly looking around for little things to put in my pockets to sell when I returned to the ship.

While looking in a particular bomb crater, I found a paper

box that had a brand new uniform, pants, coat and hat. It also had this neat looking little wooden cylinder about eight inches long and one and a half inches in diameter. I stuck it in my pocket and headed back to the boat.

When we looked at the uniform, we found that it would fit my deck hand, Sanchez, who was small and stubby with a week's growth of beard, When we hit the beach he wouldn't go ashore for anything. So we got a great idea. We put the uniform on him and when we got within sight of the ship he stood up on the stern of the boat with his hands over his head while I pointed my gun at him.

You can imagine the flurry of excitement aboard a ship as we approached with a captured Japanese soldier. I marched him up the gangway and turned him over to the officer of the deck with the story that I had just killed off a hundred Japanese all by myself and this guy was the only one left and of course I expected to be awarded the Navy Cross for my bravery in action. About that time someone recognized Sanchez, so we had to run down to our boat and get the heck out of there! To keep my head on straight, there had to be a little humor in everything that was happening. If you looked at the negative side you would lose it all, big time.

I put this little wooden cylinder down in the gunnel of the boat and forgot about it. A month or so later I found it and put it in my locker. Another couple of months went by and I happened to see it so I thought I would check it out. It had a screw top and down inside it looked like a fine watch with a lot of little brass wheels. I had no idea what it was so I took it to the chief gunners mate and he unscrewed the top and peeked inside. He turned white. He very slowly screwed the top on and handed it back to me and said to take it v-e-r-y slowly topside and throw it overboard, but wait until he had cleared the area of all people. This thing was a timer and was full of high explosives that the Japanese pilots put into large bombs to blow them up when they were within a couple hundred feet off the ground. I was sorry to lose a great souvenir. I probably could have gotten ten bucks for it.

12/10/1943 It's back to Pearl Harbor

We unloaded the 27th Army Division at Pearl and after a
short overhaul we went back to Maui. We went
through five weeks of extensive training of 200 officers and
4,000 enlisted men in the art of amphibious warfare. This
was very grueling for those of us in the boat crews. From
dawn to dark it was like going through the motions of real
assault landing on the beaches of Maui.

The mornings were clear and calm, but you could almost
set your watch by the 2:00 p.m. heavy seas and very
strong trade winds that blew down between Maui and
Molokai Islands. This meant the waves were crashing over
our boats and the winds would cut into our faces. The
poor troops in our cargo area would be tossed in all
directions, soaked from head to foot, and be terribly
seasick as well. I wore plastic rain gear but it didn't help
much. The army created a plastic face mask to protect
their tank divers from the blowing dust. I swiped a case for

my self and they worked great against the salt spray and rain. This was real misery time. No one seemed to enjoy that the rougher it got the louder I would sing.

One time during a sudden storm I dumped my troops on the beach and made a beeline for my ship. When I arrived all the boats were lifted aboard, except mine. By this time the seas were too high (a ten to fifteen foot drop), so there was no way to hook onto the davits to be lifted aboard. As a result, we circled around the ship like a baby duck in the down pour rain and wind. Finally, we just shut off the engine and drifted for miles. Then we headed back to do it all over again. The surf was too high and dangerous to land on the beach.

After several trips, the Officer of the Deck called out to us with a speaker to go to the stern of the ship. When we got there we saw a whole gang of boat crews waving and laughing at us. We were becoming quite an attraction aboard ship and I guess a sorry sight to see. They lowered a big box down on a line and I went underneath it and they dropped it into the boat. When we opened up the box the crew all yelled "Merry Christmas". It contained a whole turkey, mashed potatoes and gravy, a whole cake, hot coffee, six cold beers and three cartons of cigarettes! Again we shut down the engine and drifted while we celebrated our first Christmas at sea. Later that night the storm let up enough for us to be lifted aboard the ship.

For more than sixty years I have made my family listen to this story over and over on Christmas day.

01/01/1944 ~ Back and forth to Pearl Harbor

When we would go back to Pearl to exchange troops, we would have a few days to wander around Honolulu. I found a Chinese restaurant named Pi Y Chongs that served porter house steaks as big as your plate. There were little or no vegetables, no lettuce at all and of course very bad rum and cokes. What more could an eighteen year old sailor want.

One day I found my deck hand, Sanchez, in our landing craft aboard ship crying and cussing out the Navy loud and clear. He read me a letter he had just received from his wife from a small village in Texas saying she and their babies were sick with high fevers and diarrhea. She was too weak to lift or feed the children and they had had nothing to eat for days. She had tried to call for help, but no one could understand or listen to her. She said our country had stolen him away. She also said she loved him very much but that they were going to die now.

I took him to the wardroom where the Captain and officers were having lunch. I opened the hatch (door) and pushed him in and said "Go get the bastards". He proceeded to scream and cuss how much he hated the Navy, the Captain and the Jap's. The Skipper and the Chaplain hustled him out the door where I could tell them his story. The Skipper got on the radio with someone who knew someone in Texas. Later we were told the Red Cross had found them and that his family was doing just fine. I was told much later (after I was transferred to the Rocky Mount) that my old ship went back to San Francisco and my buddy was able to spend a week with his family. When he came back to the ship and as he stepped aboard, a guy wire snapped and a shackle hit him in the head killing him on the spot. War is Hell

Yet Another Sea Story! It's amazing what a bunch of young bored kids will do just to see if they can get away with something. Particular if you are from way down south

The masts at the front and rear of the old Pierce went all the way down to the ship's keel. They were hollow with heavy reinforcements. Two decks down in the forward second division sleeping compartment, the mast had a small inspection plate about a foot square, and it was bolted with heavy half inch bolts.

Some of the guys from down south got what they thought was a fantastic idea. They took the plate off and constructed a little shelf that would hold a hot plate, a coffeepot with tubing installed in the top that wound around, creating a still of sorts. They connected the wiring to an electric outlet on the bulkhead and painted it the same color as the wall. After bolting the inspection plate back on and pushing a bunk up against it, you couldn't see their handy work.

They cooked anything that would ferment and made up some terrible tasting stuff they were proud to call their own "white lightning". The part of the project that was really fun was that the mast had an opening at the top. When I was on watch at the steering wheel up on the bridge, the Captain was going bananas trying to figure out how there could be such a sweet smell in the air in the middle of the Pacific Ocean! If I had said anything it would have been "over the side" for me, for sure!

Gone fishing! One time I was cruising along in my boat and saw a large fish floating on the surface ahead of me. So I thought I would just run over that sucker. As I reached him, I saw that it was a tiger shark with big spots, and much to my dismay he was much larger than my boat! I slammed the boat in reverse and swerved around him sending my crew head over heels into the bottom of the boat.

We stopped to look at him and it was the largest fish I had

ever seen. In a few minutes he slowly disappeared. The concussion from our bombs exploding brought many fish to the surface. When we made our landings on the beach, there were thousands of small tropical fish floating around and we would tie a line to a bucket and pick up some to look at. They were really beautiful.

After the Invasion of Makin Island those of us who had handled landing craft were told how lucky we were. One of the other islands in the Gilbert group was named Tarawa (Betio) and as it turned out, the Japanese put their main fighting force on this island. If our ship had been chosen to invade it, none of our boats would have survived including me. They chose to make the invasion at dawn and coral reefs sticking up out of the water made it nearly impossible to reach the shoreline so our forces were sitting ducks for the Jap's to pick them off one by one. This was our first experience and to say the least, we learned that no matter how much we bombed and shelled an island, we could not penetrate the enemy's cement pill boxes, and their dug-in troops. They were ready and waiting and had to be dealt with one at a time!

Of course, the boats on top of the water made beautiful targets and we lost most of them. Later one of the boat crew coxswains was transferred to our ship and he said he spent two days in the water under his destroyed boat.

War is Hell

From Makin Island it was back to Hawaii where we picked up a new ship load of troops and off to Maui we went for a few weeks of training so the boys would know how to hit the beaches running. This was very grueling to those of us who went around and around from ship to shore in our 36 foot wooden boats (LCVP). We carried 36 men or a jeep, and of course, ammunition and food supplies. This was very boring to say the least.

The Marshall Islands
The Kawajaline Atoll

01/22/1944

Once more our fully loaded ship left Pearl Harbor into waters controlled by Japanese submarines. My duties at sea were manning the wheel on the bridge. I soon became a qualified helmsman (This is a big deal in the Navy). There are no margins for error in an invasion of maybe forty to fifty ships all swinging like snakes so as not to be a standing target for the subs. The map went up on the bulkhead wall, and we said "hello" to Kwajaline and Eniwetok Islands , the largest islands in the atoll of many in a large circle. This circle was the rim of an old volcano called the Marshall Islands.

The Marshall Islands are somewhat more than 2,000 miles southeast of Hawaii and about the same distance to the Japanese mainland to the northwest. Japan had 20,000 soldiers and 150 aircraft on the islands, and were rushing in more reinforcements. It was in our best interest to launch an attack as soon as possible. So only ten weeks after the Gilbert invasion, we went with forward with "Operation Flintlock".

The U.S. Seventh Air Force bombers flying from the Ellice and Gilbert Islands kept the Marshall's under constant attack until the landings went into high gear. By D-Day we had complete mastery of the skies over the Marshall's. Our effort was to capture the Majuro and Kwajalein Atolls. These atolls amounted to about 20 to 50 sandy reef encircled islands. Some of them are only a few hundred yards in diameter, strung out about 60 miles long with a 20-mile wide circle.

Kwajalein Island in the Marshals ~ I landed at the point
Notice the wing of a Navy SBD dive bomber

01/31/1944 ~ Here we go again

We relaxed a little when we found out our troops were not
going ashore until after a beachhead was established. We
also found that because of this, we would be assigned to
other ships to "help out as necessary"! At dawn on D-Day,
on some what choppy sea and clear day, my boat, my
motor machinist, a deck hand and I, the coxswain were
lowered to the water and took off for the ship we had been
assigned to. When we arrived, all of the boats on the ship
had already left for the beach. I was signaled to come
along side as 36 men climbed down a rope net into my
boat. The officer in charge told me they were to hit the
beach with a large tank, but they couldn't get it started. So
they decided to go in without it to keep their place in the
FIRST WAVE – YIKES - HERE WE GO AGAIN. When
you first charge to the shore you are frightened because of
the unknown. The second time you are paralyzed because
you know for sure. I took off at full speed until I caught up
with the line of boats approaching the tip of the island and
headed straight for the beach. The boats in my line were
large tank-lighters (LCM). When we got about a city block

from the beach we ran into the coral reefs. Of course, the heavy LCMs loaded with heavy tanks hit the coral first but since we were not carrying a heavy tank we went full speed to shore over the coral all by ourselves! The ships behind us were blasting the shoreline into a wall of flames and the sound of the shells a few feet overhead was deafening. We just plowed ahead bouncing off the reefs trying to reach the beach. Finally, the stern rudder of my boat was caught in the coral and we could go no further.

We were still about fifty feet from the sand, so I yelled at Sanchez to drop the ramp and then screamed at the troops "GIVE THEM HELL AND GOD BLESS YOU" and we dropped the ramp. The troops ran out straight into machine gun fire about shoulder high in the water and tried to move toward the shore through the coral reefs that were from two to ten feet deep. As the troops ran out onto the ramp of the boat, the bow went down and with weight of the troops on the forward ramp, our boat filled up with water. This left me stuck with my stern sticking up out of the water on the reef. Needless-to-say, this "one boat invasion force" got the attention of the Japanese and how

118

we survived, I'll never know. It was not one of my best days. War is Hell.

My deck hand rolled up the ramp and the three of us got down in the water inside the boat and started bailing it out with buckets. I'm sure we looked like "Old Faithful". By this time the other boats were making their landing all around us and the war was in progress. We finally bailed out enough water to float and since the engine was mid ship toward the stern, it worked fine. The rudder was smashed and the screw propeller was bent so we could only shutter in a circle. I kept going back and forth until I finally worked our way out of the coral It took what seemed like hours, but I made it along the side an LSD ship that hooked on to us and brought us aboard. I used a sledge hammer to straighten out the rudder and screw propeller the best I could, and the ship's crew put us back in the water and then we were on our way to our ship about a mile away.

When they lifted our poor old boat aboard, the first thing I heard was that the Captain wanted to see me. Reporting up to the bridge as instructed he smiled and said "Where in the hell have you been and what did you do to our boat?" Then he mumbled something I didn't understand, he asked me if I liked him and our ship. I said, "Okay, I guess so". Then he said he had a communiqué in his hand from Admiral Turner's staff on the Rocky Mount asking to transfer me to their ship – NOW! I asked if I had done something wrong and if I was in trouble?. He said he didn't know what I was doing in on the beach but apparently somebody was watching and took the number off of the bow of your boat so get going right now, and a boat would take you to this command ship. As soon as I was packed, away I went with no idea what to expect but after what I had just been through nothing would surprise me anymore

Keep your head down soldier, those guys are mad

September 15th 1944 ~ The invasion of the Island of Peleliu

Our great white fathers made the decision to pass up some of the major islands such as Truck and let them "Just wither on the vine". For some unknown reason to me, General Macarthur decided to capture the Island of Peleliu (six miles by two miles). It wasn't hurting anything. Peleliu was just lying there, but we hit the island hard with 6,526 men and lost 1,232 of them. The Japanese lost 10,000 troops --??

I did not have to go there as the Rock was getting ready for our next major invasion in the Marianas Islands. The reason I am bringing it up is that I was told that several members of the boat crews on my old ship "The Pierce" were killed at this invasion, They were my shipmates and the news really hurt me.

The USS Rocky Mount ~ AGC 3

The Rocky Mount

The Flagship AGC Rocky Mount

Displacement: 13,910 tons

Length: 459 feet

Beam: 63 feet

Draft: 24 feet

Speed: 16 knots

Compliment: 503 Armament: 2 - 5 inches and 8 – 40 mm

Class: Appalachian

The USS Rocky Mount ~ AGC 3

What it takes to do a 25 month cruise

The twenty-five month cruise traveled 48,469 miles; used 2,847,856 gallons of fuel, 18,512,000 gallons of water, 800,000 razor blades, 76,000 bars of soap and 2,100,000 cigarettes. The ship could supply the city of Los Angeles with electricity for one year using 2,647,236 kilowatts. The laundry washed and dried amounted to 907,200 pounds of clothing. Money spent for paydays was $1,532,556. Ships Store sales were $148,012 with the Small Stores sales totaling $93,040. The Photography Laboratory used 132,337 square feet of printing paper. We ate 2,307 meals using 140,000 loaves of bread cut into 3,200,000 slices, 875,000 pounds of meat, 72,500 pounds of butter, 300,000 eggs, 150,000 pounds of fruit, 250,000 pounds of fresh vegetables, 2,900,000 pounds of dry provisions. The food total was 4,295,000 pounds in all. Ammunitions expended were 806 five inch shells, 13,604 forty millimeters, 30,912 twenty millimeters and 5,610 fifty caliber projectiles. The USS Rocky Mount fought her way through nine separate operations to victory! It was tough, but someone had to do it ???

Our invasion force managed to take ashore the Army's 32nd, 184th regiments and the 7th Division. Admiral Turner
and General Smith were in charge. Kwajalein was two and a half miles long and 800 yards wide. The 5,100 Japanese troops fought for four days with no wounded and 49 prisoners. Our losses were 144 U.S. dead and 846 wounded.

Nevertheless, the U.S. triumph showed that island hopping was the best way to deliver a deathblow against the Japanese Empire. Victory in the Marshall's provided the foot hold from which landings and air craft raids could be made throughout the central Pacific, and allow the allies to accelerate their offensive at a far greater rate than had been hoped for.

02/03/1944 ~ "Good bye" to the Pierce and "Hello" to the Rock

I was soon packed and on my way to the Flagship. I didn't have time to think about leaving a whole shipload of very good friends never to be seen again, but that's the Navy way.

As our boat approached the ship, I was really confused. This was the strangest looking ship I had ever seen. The camouflage was painted to look like two ships one behind the other.

The superstructure was dominated by radio and radar gear. There were davits for seven boats. It had the look of an old supply transport. I found out later that this was a very top secret ship; a floating hotel for all the top brass from every branch of the service. The Rocky Mount did all the coordination and planning of naval and troop activity, the invasion in process and also the ones to follow. We were within sight and part of the action all the time and we were the leading ship of each attack convoy. The enemy didn't know we were there, and the kamikaze and bombers never gave us a second look.

The boat crew let me off on the gangway. I saluted the stern flag, gave the officer of the deck my records and reported aboard. The officer asked why I was there, and I answered that I didn't have the slightest idea. He said there was an invasion going on and he didn't have time to screw around with me. I told him I had heard about the invasion but not to worry, I would be just fine. I asked around and found out where the boat crew compartment was, found an empty bunk and locker and made myself at home. After a nap I found the galley and had dinner. I really liked being invisible. I took a complete tour of the ship and tried to look like I was doing something very important. This went on for several days.

Then one day I heard my name over the ship's public address system saying to report to the Officer of the Deck. He asked me where the heck I'd been and I said that I was waiting for him to find me, If he needed me, just pass the word on our public address system. He sent me up (a couple of decks) to the Flag lieutenant (CEO) who also had been looking for me. The "Flag" is the name of the support group for the presiding Admiral and is not really part of the ships crew. They go where the Admiral goes. He said he had heard I was pretty good at handling boats. I told him that I was with out doubt the best Boat Coxswain in the whole US Navy. He took me over to the side and pointed out a boat I had never seen before and asked if I could drive it. I said "no problem". I later found out that it had been converted from an old landing craft with a pointed bow, a flat bottom, 36 feet in length, a gray marine diesel engine, a cabin with windows, leather bench seats, and fancy brass railings running along the gunnels and cabin roof. The boat also had three stars on the bow and an American flag on the stern. The Lieutenant said that it was especially made for Vice Admiral Kelly Turner who was in charge of the Fifth Amphibious Force for the Pacific Ocean. He then said that when the Admiral needed his boat I was to be standing by and ready to go twenty-four hours a day. I couldn't believe the whole thing. This had to be the best duty for a sailor in the whole U. S. Navy.

I was assigned to become part of the ship's boat crews. This was a group of guys especially trained to go onto the beaches the day before the troops arrived, and report on what to expect from the enemy fortification. These guys were really tough, or crazy would be a better word. Since they were only effective the first few days of the invasion, they were used to run the seven landing crafts on the ship the rest of the time. I was given a deck hand and a motor machinist to be my crew. We became part of the ship's company even though I was responsible only to the Admiral and his flag. They didn't like it having a stranger dropped on them at all; and when I told them I was from Hollywood, I thought they were going to throw me overboard. Being from Hollywood meant that you were very rich and queer. Of course I was neither but that didn't mean anything. I still had to carn their respect and that took awhile.

Admiral Richmond Kelly Turner was a very interesting man. He was about sixty years old, and like most top level leaders in the Navy, he lived a very lonely life. He was loud and gruff, used lots of profanity and stared at you with a very intense demand for your attention. Other than General Holland Smith of the Marines, I don't think he had a friend in the world, and I'm not sure about that. At meetings he over-whelmed and terrorized those around him and always got his way because no one would dare counter his ideas. I think Admiral Turner respected me because I showed no fear and over-reacted with a smile at his orders. I think I impressed him because I was a real "Jock" when it came to operating his boat. I only knew how to go full speed ahead and make slam dunk landings.

If one of the Admirals or Generals fell down in my boat they would give me a dirty look, but the old man would laugh and tell them to get some sea legs if they wanted to be in his Navy. I was dead serious and very GI when we had anyone else in the boat. My two-man crew would follow my lead, but when we were alone, off came the hat and shirt. He knew we would play the role so he had a relaxed attitude. He loved to fish and had a full range of equipment.

He gave me a roll of fishing line and a couple of hooks and jigs that I tied to one of the stern lines. His cook fried our fish. He dreamed about hooking up with a big Marlin, so we built a seat for him in the back of the boat. We saw a few jump out of the water, but he never caught one. He would constantly get his line all tangled up and I would have to help him straighten it out. He hated that. I had to be sure we were far enough away from the other ships so that no one could see us catching fish that belonged to the Japanese.

February 22nd 1944 ~ Some sailors have real problems.

One day while aboard the "Rock", I noticed that one our boat crew deck hands sitting on his bunk holding a letter with a very perplexed look on his face. Because he was a Mexican boy I asked if I could help him, but he replied "No one can help me"! He was obviously in big trouble, so I took the letter out of his hand and read it.

I couldn't believe what I was reading. A large well known oil company in Texas was offering him a long term lease on thousands of acres of land for several thousands of dollars a month, plus so much per barrel for a large number of wells they were planning to construct on the land.

I told him if it were me, I'd sign with no questions asked! He said he thought it would be better if he waited until he went home. I said, "Are you nuts? God only knows how long we're going to be out here! Think of all the money you would be losing. What if you get killed? Think of your family!" He said he would tell me his problem if I promised for sure I wouldn't tell anyone aboard ship.

It turned out that when he was a little boy his father killed his mother, and then killed himself leaving him as the sole survivor of the family trust that owned a block of downtown San Antonio, as well as land all over the state of Texas. As a kid, he found he could not trust anyone! Everyone wanted his money, and he had no real friends. He ran away and joined a large group of Mexican fruit pickers who traveled all over the Southern states. A couple of times the word got out about him, and they would beat him up wanting some money, and girls would chase after him. He said good friends became bad friends when money came into the picture.

He said he was the happiest when no one knew about the trust, which was being managed, by his bank at home. He said he was taking a big chance on trusting me to keep my mouth shut. I had to be better than a friend ! I kept his secret, and even today when I drive down the highway and see a large group of fruit pickers out in the fields, I wonder if my old shipmate is one of those very happy, hard working folks!

02/25/1944 ~ Back to Pearl Harbor

It was time to leave that bloody island. There were no more Japanese left alive, so we raised anchor and headed back to Pearl Harbor arriving eight days later on March 3rd. I would like to say more about my time at sea, but each day was almost identical to the next. Just one heck of a lot of water as far as you can see regardless as to where you looked. Mostly hot sunshine but some times the sea would kick up a storm with winds strong enough to blow you right off of the deck and you bounced off of the bulkheads (walls) in the passage ways. You can imagine how it was to try and sleep in the racks without falling on the deck. Some times we would strip off our clothes and let the soft rainwater soak us. I was also assigned to a twenty-millimeter gun for my four-hour watch (eight hours off) and worked with the Second Division deck crew (when they could find me).

Black is Beautiful

One day I noticed this black kid leaning on the railing by himself looking out to sea with a sad look on his face so I walked up to him and said " Hey man, what's happening?" He smiled and said "Where in the world are you from?" I said, LA, California. He said "You got to be kidding me, I'm from east LA" I asked him how he was enjoying his south sea's romantic cruise and he said "I'm one miserable nigger" I said "Come on man, we don't talk that way anymore" He said " Look, I joined this mans Navy to fight a war and here I am stuck in a compartment with a bunch of uneducated blacks from down south that I can't even understand, I'm serving food to a lot of unappreciative white officers. I can't hang out with white guys like you without getting beat up. I can't go anywhere by myself. No body gave me a hint it was going to be like this and there's nothing I can do about it   I told him that I certainly understood what he was talking about but there's one thing for sure " I would be happy to meet with him anywhere anytime and just "hangout" And we did meet many times after that. He was a heck of a nice guy, I wish I could remember his name.

03/03/1944 Arrived back to Pearl

We finally reached Pearl Harbor and the Admiral went to live ashore with no need for his boat, so I just bummed around on board ship or went ashore whenever possible. I gradually made friends with the guys in the boat crews. They were a bunch of screw offs so I fit right in.

I found a large swimming pool near the air base that had a wire fence that I could climb over. There was a tower about fifty feet high just like the Olympics so I and a couple of buddies practiced diving, making believe that we were diving off of our ship when and if we were torpedoed by a lucky Japanese sub. We went there many times and no one ever tried to chase us out of there. We found out that a naked sailor looks just like a naked soldier.

03/14/1944 ~ The second Pearl Harbor Desaster

My old shipmate, John Vreeland, reminded me of a story that never made the news at home. It was termed top secret because we didn't want the enemy to know that we could be so stupid.

Shortly after returning from the Marshall Islands invasion and some training exercises, the Rock was moored to a dock at Pearl Harbor. On a very quiet Sunday morning. Liberty parties went ashore. Those that stayed aboard were making preparations for the invasion of the Marianas. This was a quiet interlude between operations. For some reason I didn't go ashore and was goofing off around on the ship.

Across the channel there were 28 LSTs nestled together at West Loch. All were fully loaded with ammunition and supplies for our next operation. Each had at least a hundred 55-gallon drums of high-octane aviation fuel on deck. Literally each one was a floating powder keg.

Suddenly there was a tremendous explosion. I ran up to the Bridge and man a twenty millimeter gun to try and see if we were being bombed by the Jap's again. Navy history tersely described it this way: The center of the blast was on the bow of LCT-963 where army troops were loading heavy mortar ammunition. High-octane gasoline on the forecastles of LST-353, 39 and 97 caught fire. There were major casualties at the center of the explosion.

A second explosion followed as more ships caught fire. Many of the sailors jumped into the water. Scores perished aboard their ships in the blazing inferno. The blast showered metal and debris over a thousand-yard radius. The smoke created a mushroom cloud that hung over the entire harbor.

Six ships and three landing craft were sunk. The human toll was appalling: 163 men died and 196 were injured. We proved once again that you never know for sure what can happen on a peaceful Sunday morning. War is hell!

Marianna Islands

Siapan Island

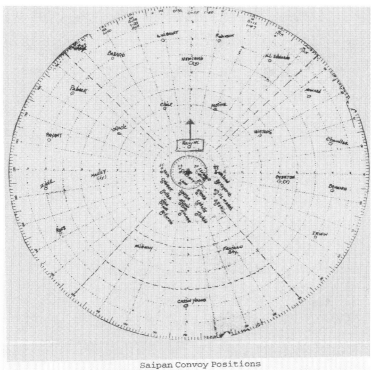

Saipan Convoy Positions
This rose was made before USS Midway was renamed USS St. Lo.
As Midway she participated in Saipan, Tinian and Morotai assaults.
USS Ballard was only on hand for Saipan.

The above "rose" is a formation that an invasion force looks like with the central troop ships being led by the Rocky Mount and all of the major fighting ships spread out

141

around us. It was exciting to look in every direction and see so much fire power.

If you stop and think about it, Everyone on those ships out there was a complete city by it's self Every shape and size. It created it's own water, electricity and all of the elements of any city needs to survive. A complete political process from the garbage grinder to the skipper. All of our ships moved together as part of the total picture of a life and death situation.

143

June 12th 1944 ~ The Invasion of Saipan in the Mariana Islands

The Mariana Islands are in the western Pacific more than 3000 miles west of Hawaii, about 1,500 east of the Philippines and some 1,000 miles north of the equator. 12 miles long with total land area is only 370 square miles, but hundreds of islands (mostly small) stretched north and south for 500 miles. At the outbreak of WWII, the total population was less than 30,000. Primary products were coffee, sugar cane, and coconuts.

5/29 1944 ~ Departed for the Marshall Islands, The first stop on the way to the Marianna's

We spent two months loading our ship with provisions for the next battle. Admiral Turner returned aboard and we set sail for the Marshall Islands to meet up with the invasion force heading for the Mariana Islands. The Fifth Fleet commanded by Admirals Spruance and Mitscher was assembled at Eniwetok in the Marshall's and we led them to Saipan. The combined force was more than 600 Fifth

Fleet ships, 127,571 troops, 30,000 garrison troops, and 1,000 Air Force planes. This made it the largest amphibious assault force mounted to date in the Pacific. Looking at ships as far as I could see in all directions gave me a feeling of confidence. It began with an air strike June 15th on Saipan. Along the way we encountered many reports of submarines in the area. We sighted rafts with about twelve Japanese who refused to be rescued, so they were left to their chosen fate.

06/15/1944 ~ Landed on the beach at Saipan

The Rocky Mount arrived at Saipan Island on the day the attack was scheduled to begin. It was during this period that Milton A. Rhea changed from a nice young boy to a tough self assured young man. Making war was just an every day thing. Many around me became mentally or physically broken but I took the position that as long as I was alive and in one piece, I would survive these horrible conditions and learn from them, making me a better man because of them. Of course, I always felt that God had his hand on my shoulder. I was not part of the initial landings this time. My duties were confined to the ship and the Admirals boat. The landings were made under heavy mortar and rifle fire as on the other islands we had just recently secured. In addition to her headquarters duties, "The Rock" cared for hundreds of casualties as a result of heavy fighting ashore.

06/18 1944 ~ The Philippine Turkey Shoot

The invasion force came to a stop when 300 planes hit us with a major air strike from a Japanese Fleet in the southwest. Our naval air force countered and shot 243 planes out of the sky. However, the Japanese sunk three of our aircraft carriers and damaged two more. This battle was called "The Philippine Turkey Shoot". There were a great number of Philippine land based planes lost and this insured the success of the Mariana operations. While this was going on the Rocky Mount wandered around in open sea until it was over.

When we arrived it was strange to see this huge barren mountain rise out of the water. We immediately began bombarding the shoreline and our landing craft established a beachhead. The battle at the shoreline wasn't very difficult because we had the full use of the Iron Ducks that carried our troops and rambled right up of the shore, but that was just the beginning of a miserable invasion for the 2nd and 4th Marine Divisions with a three star General (Howling Mad) Smith and the 27th Army division with Maj General Ralph Smith and of course my three star Admiral Kelly Turner with the Navy's 5th Amphibious Force and I must not forget 2nd class Boatsuns, Mate Milton Alexander Rhea

The Japanese were well entrenched in caves and cement machine gun bunkers. Our Navy ships bombarded the Island for three day but regardless of what our troops tried to do, the enemy was looking right down on top of them. I remember so well a group of Navy Corsair fighters diving one after the other strafing a particular location on the side of the mountain. They have wings designed after eagles and they looked so neat.

The Japanese were fierce fighters and were not very impressed with our mighty invasion force, because they could disappear into their little caves and smoke some opium and drink the last of their sake. In their minds, if they were lucky they would soon be with their ancestors "in heaven". The Japanese Navy was floating around out there somewhere and we didn't know where, but as the sun came up their aircraft would come at us in the glare of the sun. The same thing happened at sunset. They were on top of us before we could see them. We would go to "General Quarters" just before light and again just before sun down. I developed a circle on my butt from sitting on my helmet. On our regular duty it was four hours on and four hours off twenty four hour a day You are very tired all of the time.

I was not part of the boat crews landing on the beach this time (Thank God) as my duties were standing watch on the 20-millimeter gun aboard ship and operating the Admiral's boat when he wanted to go somewhere. The attacks from the air were constant. There were 32 calls to general quarters during our stay there. This is easy to write about, but living through it is something anyone would love to forget! The pressure to wait day in and day out to be killed is very exhausting! One overriding factor was you thanked God that you were not on the beach next to a Marine in a little foxhole. Unless you were right there experiencing the horrors there was no way for anyone to know or feel what it was really felt like. War is hell.

Standing at the wheel in my cabin on the boat gave me an insight that no one else had of what a real war is all about. The Admirals and Generals had to make hard and fast decisions on the spot. From their point of view the only way to win this battle was to completely overwhelm the enemy with our manpower regardless of how many lives were lost on both sides. I remember so well saying to myself, "What in the hell is the big hurry? We have them completely surrounded It was the "Rosy the Riveters, the "4Fs in the factories and the guts of our young boys that provided our great leaders with so much power. To the average sailor these men were like Gods, but to me they were just a bunch of old men who were used to getting their own way (by rank). I'm sure they thought they were doing what was best, they had never fought a war before and it was knock down and drag out time and winning by intimidation. I was amazed at how they talked to each other and for sure, they could care less about the orders coming out from Washington.

They would make a plan to cover for each other if there was a problem. I have told many negative stories about these great war heroes but no one wants to hear or believe me, but my answer is~

"Trust me, my friend, I was there"

My solution (Nobody asked me?) Was to surround the island with our Big guns and dive bombers and in a short time destroy anything that moves. When they run out of food, water, fuel and ammunition they solved their own problems by committing suicide. Good planning, right. I would have made one hell of an Admiral.

Dumping thousands of young boys on the beach to be

slathered when you have completely incapacitated the enemy in the first place bothers me. But what do I know,

I'm just a sailor ~ Yo,Ho Ho and a bottle of Rum

Taking the Admiral to the beach and to his meetings on other ships as well as picking up the top brass for the high level daily planning on our boat was an on-going duty that gave me the opportunity to get to know them on an informal basis. We would chat about the fighting, weather, food, but mostly about my boat. It would usually take about a half an hour to get from one place to the next. They would shake my hand and talk to me in a casual friendly way. This was something I wasn't used to as a sailor with the run of the mill officers in the Navy.

The Winning Team: Admiral Halsey (above left) rotated command of the fleet with Admiral Spruance (center), and Admiral Turner (above right) commanded amphibious operations. The Battle of the Philippine Sea (below) on

Strategic Decisions: The navy's mid-Pacific offensive and devastating submarine campaign (above) were defeating Japan by mid-1944. But MacArthur argued successfully for a Philippine invasion at the July conference with Roosevelt and Nimitz (below) at Pearl Harbor.

These gentlemen included Admiral King from Washington, Admiral Nimitz (the Pacific Fleet Commander), Admiral Halsey (the Carrier Commander, Admiral Kincade, Admiral Spruance, Admiral Mitscher and of course my Admiral Turner (the head of the Seventh Fleet Amphibious Force).

Also included was General Smith, I think they realized that I was the commander of the boat they were riding in (HA)

When Admiral Turner would go to a cruiser or battleship for a meeting he would always tell the officer of the deck to see that his boat crew was properly fed. That meant the chief cook would have to roll out and prepare a breakfast or dinner for us after they had cleaned the stoves and trays like new. The cooks work most of the night and sleep during the day so he would try to tell us to get lost. but being the smart ass that I was, I would order the whole works and I would remind him that I might have to take my meal on a tray to show the Admiral what a tremendous cook he was and get the approval of his ships Captain also.

I didn't often get a chance to show off so I would make the most of it when ever I got the opportunity. .

MILT's BOSS

The Feud on the Second Deck: Admiral Turner (above left), appointed by Admiral Stark (above center) as director of war plans, fought DNI Captain Kirk (above right) for control of cryptanalytic information. After Admiral Wilkinson (below left) became DNI in October 1941, Turner vetoed all operational dispatches from Commander McCollum (below center) and DNC Admiral Leigh Noyes (below right). NAVAL HISTORICAL CENTER

Sometimes a kid can get to smart for his own good. I made a trip to shore with Admiral Turner to see Marine General (Howling mad) Smith on the front lines early one morning. When we got to this old rock pier sticking out from the beach, the Admiral just walked away without saying anything as to what his plans were. So, we waited and we waited and we waited.

We sat there for awhile but as the sun got hotter (I mean real hot and very sticky), the big green flies from the decomposing bodies became extremely thick in our cabin. So I would take a run out into the bay to clear them out and float around waiting for the old man to return. Finally, about two o'clock I decided to find the Admiral and see if he was going to return soon or should we go back to the ship for lunch and some water. Then I would return later whenever he was ready. (Made sense ?).

As I wandered around looking for him I noticed a blown up bank with island money lying about, a Jap rifle and stuff to take back to the ship. There was no Admiral to be seen, so I went back to the boat to continue waiting and I wasn't

155

too happy about that. When I got back to the rock pier, my boat was gone!!! There was an Army officer in charge of the dock. He asked if my name was Rhea and when I said yes, he suggested that the front lines were just a couple of miles away and if I was lucky the Jap's would let me join up with them. He asked if I realized I had kept a General and an Admiral waiting in all of this heat and flies for over a half an hour!!! I think I'm supposed to arrest you, but I wouldn't know what to do with you.

I told him "not to worry", I could handle the old man. There was a landing craft tied to the dock and the coxswain had heard of the conversation and said he would take me out to my ship if I promised not to tell anyone. When we got to the ship we approached from the blind side of the ship that had no gangway, but had some of our boats tied up. So I slipped into one of the boats unnoticed and skimmed up a rope latter to the main deck. The guys in my crew didn't even want to talk to me. They said the Admiral told the officer of the deck that I had deserted him and to put me in the brig if he saw me.

I told the officer of the deck "not to worry" I can handle the old man?? I went up to the Admiral's deck and found the Flag Lieutenant and told him how the admiral had deserted his starving boat crew with no water or food, and that I had tried to find him. He said that I was actually a member of the ship's' company and not a member of the "Flag", so he wouldn't touch me with a ten-foot pole.

So, I went down to the bridge and asked to see the Captain. I told him my very sad story and he said this was a very serious situation and he would put me on report. He said I would have to come before a Mast (ships court) and until then I was restricted to the ship and not to go anywhere. (Where was I going to go?) Then he started to laugh and said, "Do you mean you really left the Admiral and General in all those flies and heat?" I said "yes sir". He laughed again and said "Get out of here".

My good buddies told me I was sure to get a firing squad or at least 20 years in Goat Island prison because there was nothing on the books as bad as this charge. I told them that if there was nothing on the books, they couldn't charge me with anything. About a week later I went to a very official court proceeding on the bridge with the Captain and his staff standing there. I noticed that the Admiral was on the next deck up and was watching over the railing. I again told them my sad story and they looked at each other smiling. They said this was very serious and the Captain said I was to be restricted to the ship for three months. It was common knowledge that the Admiral and Captain didn't get along so I really lucked out.

My deck hand tried to operate the boat and he ripped all of the railing off the gunnels on the side of the boat making a landing. The next day I was called to report to the Admiral's cabin. He told me to continue operating the barge and that from now on when he said wait, I dammed sure better wait. And I said, YES SIR, Admiral !!!

While many ships around us were strafed, the Rock came through untouched. I guess our ship didn't look like it was worth the effort. While we were being attacked one day a Jap dive bomber was diving on our ships and hit a loading boom on a ship near by and flipped over into the sea. Our

Admiral immediately sent an accommodation to the captain for being the only ship in our invasion force to knock a dive bomber out of the sky with his loading boom. Even the old man had a sense of humor now and then.

Saipan was secured July 9th. U.S. losses for the four weeks were 3,143 killed, 12,208 wounded and 335 missing. The original Japanese 31,600 had been annihilated. Only 1,800 prisoners were taken and in later mopping up operations, hundreds more were killed or captured in the hills and caves. 22,000 civilians were killed or committed suicide jumping off the cliffs. I didn't see them but some of my boat buddies were so sad after seeing all of the bodies floating in the ocean.

During the first few days of an invasion, many of our troops that had been badly wounded were brought aboard our ship for treatment because of our fine medical sick bay. Many of these men died. They were put in a canvas bag with a heavy five-inch shell at their feet to be sure that they would sink.

If we were at sea, late at night, the Chaplain would ask

some of us to help him and we would mount the soldier on a board connected to the ships railing with an American Flag over him. The Chaplain would then give a short prayer service. We would lift up the end of the board, and the soldier would slide off and drop into the sea. This was done solemnly and with the greatest of respect.

If we were anchored, we would take the soldiers in their canvas bags down the gangway to one of our boats, and then take them ashore to be buried on the island. On one such occasion, I took a couple of soldiers in their bags to shore at the island of Saipan. The marines backed up a dump truck to the boat and our boat crew lifted the heavy bags up and slid them on to the bed of the truck to be transported to the burial grounds. One of the marine bags was not tied very tightly, so when I lifted up the end of the bag, it bent in the middle.

When I slid the bag onto the truck bed, I let loose and the body fell back and what was obviously a head, hit the edge of the truck bed with a real shuddering crack! Feeling stupid, I laughed out loud at this terrible sound and I looked around to see several filthy, dirty marines laying on the ground resting from their time spent on the front lines. I went into shock as I saw the look of hatred on the faces of these men who knew this Marine could have very easily been one of them. I started to shake like a baby, because I suddenly realized that with death all around me, I had become ever so hardened! I had accepted death as an every day thing! I prayed to God that I would never again lose sight of the love I feel for my fellow man in this crazy complicated world. War is hell.

Chow Down

On the second deck up was the ships incinerator where all of our trash was burned at night and the guy that operated it was a buddy so we got to thinking that the large flat area on the top of it would make a great cooking stove when it was red hot. We made a top secret plan and slowly swiped from the galley a couple of large frying pans, pounds of butter and large stakes that were really good. We cleaned out a trash barrow and stored all sorts of good stuff for our late night dinners. One day we heard that the next day the

Captain was going to inspect our area. That night everything went over the side.

When the Captain made an inspection he was known to go bananas over a rusty screw

Take the Captain to his Ship, Coxswain   Yes sir: says I. It was a nice clear day, but there was a hurricane over the horizon somewhere causing huge rolling waves crashing on the Saipan Island shores while the bloodiest fighting was going on. The Flag Lieutenant called and asked me to take a Captain to this ship and so off we went. When I asked where his ship was, He pointed out to a little speck on the horizon. He said he had been assigned to take command of this aircraft carrier and they were waiting for him over there. So I said, okay let's go, but you had better hang on, Sir. You need to understand that when you're plowing through those huge rolling waves you have to gun the engine as you climb up the wave; at the top you spin the boat and cut the engine and slide on an angle down the back of the wave. This is so you don't plow directly into the next wave at the bottom of the swell. If you do, the next wave will crash on top of you and sink the boat. The problem is that other than me no one knows what I'm doing. They just see walls of water as they are tossed from the bottom of the trough to the crest of the wave, and back down to the trough and this can be very terrifying for those going along for the ride.

After about two hours we approached his ship. I told him that I was a qualified helmsman and it must be thrilling to handle that monster of a ship in a real storm. He said he has never been as sick and frightened in his entire naval career, and all he wanted was to get the hell out of my boat to the safety of that big ship.

As we approached the ship I could see that we had a real problem. The ship had dropped a gangway ladder down the side of the ship, and the waves were rising about ten feet above the landing. If I managed to get him on the landing the next wave would drown him.
I cruised around the ship until I spotted a small boom that was used for loading supplies. I yelled and with sign

language I finally got a boatswains mate to lower a boatswains chair down the side of the ship (this is what they use to sit on when the sides of the ship are painted). I asked him to stop the chair just above the top of the swells.

My two crew members stood on the stern of the boat with the Captain between them. As I timed the waves I brought the boat under the chair and as we rose up, my crew pushed him into the chair. The boat dropped leaving him high and dry. I gunned the engine and shot out from underneath him. All went well except the next wave was a big one and the man running the boom wasn't quick enough so the Captain was dunked in about five feet of water. I think you could have heard the carriers crew scream with laughter all the way to California. As they raised him up, I saluted him and he saluted back and said "Thank you coxswain". We lost several carriers after that I can't remember the name of the ship, I sure hope this one wasn't among them.

July 5th 1944 ~ The Silent Wounded

When we think of our wartime experience we usually start by sorting out all of those times we were subject to the possibility of immediate death, bombings, torpedoes and drowning. At the time we didn't allow ourselves to think too much about it because it was a way of life that went with the territory. But there were other types of pressures that caused more pain than some of us could handle.

For instance, one day I remember finding one young kid in our division standing back on the fantail crying his eyes out, and saying that he just wanted to die! I tried to console him with the fact that what we were doing wasn't going to last much longer, and we all would soon be going home. He handed me a letter from his neighbor reporting that his blind mother (living alone) had allowed a dirty looking young man with long hair and a beard to move into his home, and was cashing checks signed by his mother! Also, this guy was driving HIS car around town. He assured me there was no one at home to help him.

The next day I found him raving about "the German

bombers that were after us and Hitler was going to kill us all!! I took him to sickbay where they secured him to a bunk. He wasn't dangerous, but he wouldn't mind anyone unless I told him to. (He was used to taking orders from me.) How do you reason with or help someone who is not "bleeding", but has just moved on to a different world and just stares at you with a smile on his face? The last time I saw him they were taking him ashore in a straight jacket.

July 6th 1944 ~ Commander Lieutenant General Saito
Let me show you how a military leader takes responsibility, regardless of what or whose side he represents. I think they all learned how to fight a war from the same book.

Now hear this ~
THE FOLLOWING IS IMPORTANT, BE SURE AND READ

The following is a copy of the last order of Saipan's Commander Lieutenant General Saito, which he gave to

166

his officers and men defending the island of Saipan. Saito delivered this order at approximately eight hundred hours on the morning of July 6th at 10:00 a.m., just prior to his committing suicide that day.

General Saito "I am addressing the officers of the Imperial Army of Saipan".

For more than twenty days since the American devils attacked, the officers, men and civilian employees of the Imperial Army and Navy on this island have fought well and bravely. Everywhere they have demonstrated the honor and glory of the Imperial forces. I expected that every man would do his duty. Heaven has not given us the opportunity. We have not been able to utilize fully the terrain. We have fought in unison up to the present time, but now we have no materials with which to fight and our artillery for attack has been completely destroyed. Our comrades have fallen one after the other. Despite the bitterness of defeat, we pledge "seven lives to repay our country". The attack of the enemy is being continued even though we occupy only a corner of Saipan. We are dying without valor under violent shelling and bombing. Whether we attack or whether we stay where we are, there is only death. However, in death there is life. We must utilize this opportunity to exalt true Japanese manhood. I will advance with those who remained to deliver still another blow to the American devils and leave my bones on Saipan as a bulwark to the Pacific.

As it says in the Senjinkun battle ethics, 'I will never suffer the disgrace of being taken alive, and I offer up the courage of my soul and calmly rejoice in living by that eternal principal.' Here I pray with you for eternal life of the Emperor and welfare of the country. I advance to seek out the enemy. Follow me."

A **Knockout Blow:** Admiral Yamamoto (above right—a pos'
ing Roger Pineau rescued from Japan in 1949) believed a'
Admiral Nagumo (above left) was the best chance for Ja'
included powerful 10,000-ton cruisers (below)—to win a qu'
United States.

I am sure there are many who will salute and say; "There
goes a man of honor who gave his life for his country".

Well, I'm one sailor that hopes General Saito's murderous bones rots in hell. When he looked out to sea on June 15th, 1944 and saw our war ships and transports as far as his eyes could see in all directions, it was time for him to say:

"This is hopeless, and for the sake of all of the wonderful souls on this island, the only honorable thing to do is recognize the obvious and offer our surrender to the enemy. Because of his ridiculous pride (and we will never know for sure), There were 45,000 Japanese killed and 17,000 American casualties with 4,000 killed.

The following are excerpts from a statement from the Imperial General Headquarters on July 18th regarding the fall of Saipan Island.

This defeat meant the Americans and their Allies had breached the inner reaches of the Japanese Empire. Something that Tojo's militarists had promised would never happen. The direct result was the fall of the Tojo government which collapsed in the total lack of confidence now shown by the emperor and the men around him, and also the military." This communiqué was one of the most important ever issued by the Imperial Headquarters. Inherent in its sentences is the story of Japan's war against the Allies going badly, with virtually no cooperation between army and navy despite all of the brave words. And to a careful reader, it was apparent that in July 1944, the Imperial Headquarters knew the war was lost and it was warning the Japanese people. Again, quoting; "In the early part of June, a powerful task force of the enemy approached east of the Mariana Islands. On June 11th, Saipan Island was subject to air attacks by an aggregate total of 200 planes, while on June 14th, the neighborhood of the Oreai Airfield on the southwestern coast of the island was furiously bombarded with ships' guns. The main force of the enemy that appeared near the place of landing, consisted of around a dozen aircraft carriers, eight battleships and about 70 large transports."

"Before daybreak on June 15th the enemy commenced a terrific bombardment with ships' guns and aircraft and at about 7:00 a.m., under it's cover, sent about 300 landing barges over the water in an endeavor to effect a wholesale landing near Oreai on the southwest coast of the island. The Japanese units stationed on the island gave battle and more than once bent the enemy back after inflicting heavy losses, but past noon a part of the enemy force managed to secure a foothold near Cape Susup and afterwards gradually extended it. Braving the razing bombing and gunfire of the enemy tanks by attacking at close quarters. Relying on sheer weight of numbers and volume, however, the enemy came on and his strength reached a whole division."

"On June 16th, because of our terrific attacks, the enemy was almost entirely unable to extend his foothold. Day and night the Japanese units carried out attacks from the north and east part of them breaking through as far as Cape Suup, thereby cutting enemy in two, south and north, throwing them into utter confusion! But with the dawn, the enemy bombardment became so fierce that the defenders were compelled to withdraw."

(I remember this action very well). General Holland

Smith directed three divisions, Marine, Army in the middle and Marines on the out side, to charge above the city of Garapan. The loss of life was very heavy so that the Army General Ralph Smith held up so he could use his heavy artillery. But the Marines continued to move forward leaving a large gap in the middle. This allowed the Jap's to counter attack the Marines from the rear and sides. General Howlin Smith and Admiral Turner talked it over in my boat and decided to cover their back side and blame the Army for the screw up and demanded that Washington transfer two Army Generals back to Hawaii. All hell broke out because a Marine General had never demoted an Army General before and the Army refused to fight for Gen. H. Smith in the future. Once more General Smith and Admiral Turner showed no regard for the lives of our troops. We made some really stupid moves! If the General had asked me, I could have saved these troops! When I listened to them making plans, I said to myself, "These guys are out of their cotton picking minds." Yeah!

More Quotes from General Saito:

"Thereafter, damage to our side gradually increased under frenzied bombings of enemy aircraft and gunfire. Beginning on about June 19th, the defending force was compelled to adjust its front line at the center between the town of Garapan Laulau Bay. Since June 20th the enemy was using the Oreai airfield. The same day the Aslito airfield field fell as well into enemy hands."

"About June 23rd or 24th the sources of water on Saipan Island had been completely destroyed, and it became extremely difficult to obtain any water supply.

"Furthermore the enemy, in command of the air and sea supremacy, daily intensified warship bombardment and air attacks which eventually covered the whole island. For ten days following the enemy landings on the island, the Japanese fought bravely day and night. Unfortunately the losses on our part considerably increased, and the movement of our troops (not to mention night assaults), were rendered difficult by the search lights from the war ships and also by flare bombs."

"Until the evening of June 25th the Japanese force maintained the line linking Garapan at the southern foot of Mt. Tapochau and Donnie. But due to the onslaught of the enemy units supported by tanks, the firing line became entangled at about this time. Undaunted in the face of such furious fighting, the Japanese troops charged into the enemy (some with bombs under their arms) to the great terror of the opponents." In addition, it was my observation that many soldiers tied their bayonets to bamboo poles and charged our troops!)

"On the night of June 26th, Mt. Tapochau fell into enemy hands. Since Mt. Tapochau is the highest peak on Saipan, the enemy immediately established powerful artillery on the southern side of the height. Thus the war situation became unfavorable for the Japanese. From June 28th on,
the enemy attacks became further intensified, and the Japanese were forced into a state where all guns were destroyed and all ammunition was exhausted. Despite such a predicament, our forces kept on fighting, and part of our units were still holding firmly to points in the southern

sectors of Mt. Tapochau preventing the enemy a northward advance. As the war situation became further aggravated, the Imperial Japanese force (displaying their characteristic bravery) continued their terrific attacks against the enemy. Some of our soldiers had no water to drink for three days, while some kept on fighting, eating leaves and even snails. "Thereupon about 3000 wounded men, who could not rise due to their wounds, voluntarily ended their own lives. All important papers were burned and destroyed. At night the final order to attack was given. Subsequently, they fell back to their cavern defense for about ten days, until finally they reddened the soil with their blood!"

"Yes, in response to the shouts of the officers and men who sacrificed themselves for eternal justice with smiles on their faces they believed in sure victory for Nippon. We will, without fail, display the glorious tradition of the Imperial Forces and profoundly pledge we will annihilate the enemy if the arrogant enemy approaches the mainland of Nippon."

As the record shows, that night General Saito ordered out

the last of the delicacies he had saved in the command cave. He and his staff ate canned crabmeat and drank sake. He excused himself saying that he wanted to sleep until just before dawn, when he would personally lead the last banzai charge into the teeth of death. But he did not. He went to his secluded spot in the command cave and committed seppuku. Admiral Nagumo committed seppuku also. See I told you so ~ What can I say? Today, General Saito, his troops and the civilians on that miserable little island could be joining all the Japanese lying on the sand in front of the Royal Hawaiian Hotel on Wakiki Beach. And they might be one of the many hundreds of happy Japanese who are saying to themselves: "Ahh So, These Amellicans are not so bad all after all. What caused all this unhappiness?"

07/21/1944 ~ Guam Island

Next was Guam Island more than 100 miles to the south of Saipan. This was a large island covered with a thick layer of jungle growth and not as heavily protected as Saipan so we were able to secure this island in about three weeks.

Guam was three times the size of Saipan and was defended by 18,500 Japanese. Two separate landings were carried out on July 21st, 1944 and 25,000 troops were
ashore by evening. On August 11th the battle was far from over. All of the Japanese forces were killed except those that hid out in the jungle, some for decades. U.S. losses on Guam ran to 7,800 dead including 245 sailors, 838 soldiers and 6,716 Marines. I remember well the day we started getting flash signals in the jungle well down the coast asking for help. We sent one destroyer and a landing craft, and very carefully picked up a sailor named Tweedy off of the beach, He had been hiding in caves that the jungle had covered up for three years. The local natives supplied him with food during this time. He looked pretty good considering what he went through.

07/24 1944 ~ Tinian Island

Meanwhile, on July 24th the first landings were made on Tinian Island. Tinian was three and a half miles north of Saipan. It was mostly level, so we enlarged the airfield to accommodate our latest machine, the B29, so now we could bring the war directly to Japan's homeland. Our only problem was we were still too far away to provide fighter aircraft protection for the bombers. This was solved with the invasions of islands closer to Japan.

Eight thousand Japanese defended Tinian. Although the fighting was furious, it was virtually over in nine days. U.S. losses were 328 killed and 1,571 wounded. In contrast, the Japanese garrison was completely wiped out. I think that about this time, these Marines were really mad.

So now we have just completed one of the major steps toward victory over a very tough adversary. It was time to go back to Pearl Harbor, settle down and plan our next steps in this horrible war led by very determined fanatics.

09/15/1944 Depart for Hawaii

The Rocky Mount completed one of the major steps toward

victory as controlling flag ship for this whole operation and we were happy to depart for Hawaii and tie up in Pearl Harbor 11 days later. (It's a big ocean out there, but it was nice to get some rest.)

I didn't give it much thought at the time but when Admiral Turner took his staff off of the ship he didn't come back aboard and since I was part of the ships company I didn't go with him. I think that if he would have thought about it he would have transferred me to his flag. Maybe he was still mad at me for leaving him on the beach.

08/ 26/ 1944 ~ Our Skipper lost it big time

Our crew will remember when the Rock tried to land along side a dock in Pearl Harbor and the skipper "lost it". Apparently, he misjudged the wind. As we eased up to the dock and tossed out our hawsers to secure to the cleats on the dock, he cut the engines and we started to drift very slowly away from the dock and across the slip. The hawsers started to sing as they stretched tight and the boatswain's mate had to let out the line to keep it from snapping. There was a very light breeze, but the side of a ship is like a huge sail. With the engines off we could not stop the drifting, and with the slow glide the lines had to be let out. There is nothing more dangerous than to have a mooring line break, as it can cut a person right in half when it snaps like a whip!

As we drifted across the slip, I could see we were in big trouble! Across the slip was a Merchant Marine ship docked and the crew was yelling at us to keep coming. I didn't understand this until later.

It seemed like it took forever to drift across, so I climbed up on a gun mount to "watch the show". I fully expected we would ease up to the other ship, bounce off, and would tie up along side until we could find a tug boat to push us back where we belonged.

Well, I was amazed! Even though we were moving ever so

slowly when we made contact with the other ship, steel railings, gun mounts and anything that protruded was ripped away like butter. The noise was like an unbearable screaming! It was shocking to say the least.

Just for fun I shook hands with a sailor on the other ship, and he said "This is great! We'll be stuck here for months while they repair this mess". Then I understood the "beauty" of the entire happening.

A tug finally showed up to push us back to our own dock. It took quite awhile to repair the damage, so it was off to Wakiki Beach every day. "Tough duty!" We had one embarrassed Captain!

09/10/1944 ~ Flying is for the birds

There is only so much to do around Honolulu, so one must be a little creative to fill the time you have on liberty. One day I went walking and found myself over at Hickham Field watching the planes take off and land. I soon found myself in the Head Operations Office. In a conversation with a pilot I learned that a pilot had to fly at least four hours a month in order to receive flight pay. So the pilots who were stationed on the base had to check out a plane and fly somewhere around the island at least once a month. There was a couch by the wall, so I would sit there and read a magazine until I overheard a pilot making a flight plan. If he was going to return the same day, I would ask if I could go along just for fun. In most cases he would say "sure because it's very boring to be up there by yourself for long periods of time". I did this many times, as flying around the islands was really an interesting way to spend some time.

On one particular flight in a B26 to Maui, I sat up in the nose where the bombardier normally sat. Now that was a real thrill! The plane is behind you and you feel like you're all by yourself, flying along through the sky like super man. As we cruised along I suddenly noticed that a little island down below me was bouncing up and down. I looked back at the pilot and he gave me the thumb pointing to the back of the plane. When I got back to the large cabin, there were three Air Force ground crew men strapping on their

parachutes and were preparing to jump out of an open
bomb bay door in the deck. They told me we were losing
an engine and it was leaking oil and might catch on fire at
any second, and they wanted out of there. Looking down
at the ocean there was a Navy destroyer that looked as big
as a match stick that could pick us up so I asked where
the parachutes were and they answered that each man
had his own and that was it! They suggested I take the
one away from the pilot because he was going to try to fly
back. When I asked the pilot for his chute he said not to
worry because he thought we could make it back to Pearl
So I asked what would happen if he was wrong, he said,
"We would then make a different plan." Until then no one
would be allowed to jump. We shuttered along, sometimes
on one engine, and all the time the ground crew guys were
complaining about staying in the plane. This experience
gave me a strange feeling in my stomach and a very alert
mind set!

We all think we know ourselves quite well until we find our
selves in a very critical or unusual situation. All the time I
sat there with the three ground crew men, I was wondering
which one of these fine gentleman was going to "donate"

his parachute to me if the plane caught on fire. I think they read my mind because they wouldn't talk or even look at me. When we landed they had a fire truck out on the landing strip. When I left the plane everyone laughed and shook my hand, and with a stupid grin, they suggested that I stay on the ground.

Thereafter, I spent my liberty time on the sandy beach in front of the Royal Hawaiian Hotel with a rum and coke in my hand.

09/10/ 1944 ~ We are on our way to the Philippines with several stops along the way.

To understand the war effort in the Philippines, one really has to start at the beginning of the whole thing. So be patient with me.

President Roosevelt made the journey to Hawaii to meet with Admiral King, Admiral Nimitz, and General MacArthur on July 26th, 1944. King and Nimitz felt that we could neutralize the airfields and control the seas around the islands and bypass the whole country. MacArthur was up in arms because he had personally promised the Philippines people that "HE would return".

Roosevelt was up for re-election and MacArthur convinced him that the people would be real unhappy if we didn't keep our word and return to save them. So once again the decisions were made on a political basis rather than number of lives that could be saved.

We build them faster then anybody

Because of the unbelievable skills of our pilots and the fantastic industrial strength of our country, the tide had turned. We now had 12 battleships, 32 carriers, 23 cruisers, 100 destroyers, 1,400 aircraft and 430 transports. The Japanese had 7 battleships, 4 carriers, 2 battle/carriers, 20 cruisers and 29 destroyers.

09/15/1944 ~ Rear Admiral Forrest B Royal and his flag boarded the Rock

On September 15th, Rear Admiral Forrest B. Royal

boarded with his Flag and took command of the Amphibious Group Six. He was very easy going and easy to get along with. I liked him very much. After some ship repairs, we set sail for the island of Manus that had recently been captured by passing one of Japan's major bases in the area, Rabaul. This cut Japan's supply line to the islands to the south.

Admiral Halsey on the New Jersey was all set to invade Mindanao, but his pilots said the place was already destroyed so he went for the Leyte Gulf. On September 15th we left Pearl for the Manus Island where we collected supplies and cleaned up the ship, and made ready for the Invasion Leyte Gulf.

King Neptune
Takes Command of the U.S.S. Rocky Mount

TO ALL SAILORS WHEREVER YE MAY BE: .... *and to all Mermaids,Whales, Sharks, Sea Serpents, Porpoises, Dolphins, Eels, Skates, Suckers, Crabs, and all other Living Things of the Sea!* KNOW YE:......*That on this 1st day of October 1944 there appeared within Our Royal Domain the U.S.S. Rocky Mount bound south for the Equator and for a base in the South Pacific.* BE IT REMEMBERED: *that said vessel and crew thereof have been inspected and passed by ourself and Royal Staff.* AND BE IT KNOWN: *By all ye Sailors, Marines, Land Lubbers and others who may be honored by his presence that* ⟨...⟩ *⟨...⟩ having been found worthy to be numbered as one of our Trusty Shellbacks he has been duly initiated into the:* SOLEMN MYSTERIES OF THE ANCIENT ORDER OF THE DEEP *Be it further understood: That by virtue of the power vested in me I do hereby command all my subjects to show honor and respect for him wherever he may be.* DISOBEY THIS ORDER UNDER PENALTY of OUR ROYAL DISPLEASURE.

Given under our hand and seal on this 1st day of October 1944

Davey Jones ~ Neptunus Rex
His Majesty's Scribe ~ Ruler of the Raging Main

I'm painting their stomachs with my crud
Notice my boat in the background

A kid with his hairy chest (and head) and his bucket of crud

Check out Hollywood with all that hair

10/01/1944 ~ The Rock Crossed the Line

During the voyage to Manus, we crossed the equator and this
This caused a very serious major event in the Navy. The
whole world stops and the Shellbacks (sailors that have been
across before) and Pollywogs (sailors that are crossing for
the first time) create a fantastic memory. Of the 800 or so
aboard ship there were only about 50 that were Shellbacks,
so we only had a short time to put the program together. (I
went across on the way to the Gilberts on the USS Pierce).
We met every day for planning in the mess hall. It's amazing
what the devious minds of a bunch of sailors can come up
with.

The uniform of the day was skivvy shorts only and bare
feet.(100 degree metal decks) They first faced me and I
painted their chests black crud that I collected from down in
bilges.

They bowed on their knees to King Neptune. They danced
on the 150-degree deck for the Queen while being stuck with
pitchforks that were rigged with electric shock points.

They had to get down and kiss the royal three hundred-pound baby's belly. They were operated on. A huge knife from a bucket of ice laid on their stomachs and catsup poured all over them with a spoonful of alum put in their mouths. They just knew that they were cut up. Next was to crawl down a line of shell backs beating them with canvas covered clubs. The royal barber cut off half of their hair. The barber's chair was connected to the deck railing so you lifted the foot up and dumped the pollywog backwards over the rail to about a 15 foot drop into a 10 X 10 canvas bag full of salt water. They were pushed down till they choked.

They were then pushed into a canvas tunnel about fifty feet long jammed with the week's garbage. On the opposite end a fire hose pushed them back into the tube. They had to stand in line by rank and believe it or not Admiral Forrest B. Royal had never been across before and was first in line. I told him that now was payback time for all of the dirty, rotten and miserable no good things he had done to us poor swabbies, and I gave him a big swipe across the chest with a 12 inch paint brush full of black bilge crud. You should have heard the screams that went up from the hundreds that were watching. (He was a good sport) There were a lot of bruised sailors, but everybody had a memory never to be forgotten, but that's OK, you are a Shell Back now! The Rocky Mount went back to winning a war.

10/05/1944 Manus Island for supplies

While awaiting the invasion of the Philippians our ship spent some time at the Island of Manus that had a large protected bay. Our forces had captured the island some time before our arriving in the area. When we entered the bay, you could tell something was wrong by the lack of activity on the several ships anchored there. We soon found out that a couple of days before we got there an ammunition ship blew up. A whole ship just disappeared and caused a lot of damage to surrounding ships. We were really lucky to have not been there at that time.

I spotted a small LST ship that had one of my high school buddies on it. That night I went over to see him and was surprised to see no one on deck. I went aboard and found everyone asleep and I mean everyone. I searched around and found my buddy and woke him up. He said it was great to see me, but he wasn't up to socializing. It seemed that the crew broke into a shipment of pure alcohol. They mixed it with pineapple juice and it wasn't long before everyone aboard was passed out. Oh! the joy of serving on a small ship.

Want to buy a beer?

Our boat crews on the ship (before I was transferred to them) were part of a trained scout and raider group. (Hand to hand fighting) One of the reasons we were left alone to do our own thing was that everyone was afraid they might get angry and kill them

One night we had a chance to put their vast experiences to work. We raided the officer's recreation area and stole several cases of beer and put them safely under the floorboards of our boats. This was top secret stuff but it was difficult to find reasons to get buckets of ice from the galley without anyone wondering why.

Anyone want to buy a boat?

On one of my frequent side trips I spotted a small native village, so naturally I investigated to see what was going on. It was a real for sure native village. The people lived in little palm branch huts, just sitting around doing nothing that I could see. They were very black with a mass of curly hair; their mouths had few teeth and were bright red from chewing some kind of narcotic nuts or berries. They were naked except the women wore a cloth belt worn to keep their boobs from flopping.

We stayed on our boat and watched. A little boy about six or seven years old was playing with a very interesting carved sailboat in the water beside us. Our motor mac, Mercer, asked the boy if he could buy the boat. The boy just looked at us with big brown eyes and said nothing. Mercer took out a couple of dollars and showed the boy the money and pointed at the boat, still nothing. Then Mercer added a couple more dollars and more sign language. Still there was no sign of understanding from the boy. I told Mercer to forget it. Obviously the boy didn't understand our language. Finally the boy yelled, "Hey dad, this guy wants to buy my boat. What do you think it is worth?" A big old black guy said, "Tell him that there is a store about a block away where he can buy his own boat. We rolled on the deck with laughter and for months after we asked Mercer if he knew where we could buy a boat. He didn't think we were very funny.

Leyte Gulf
Lingayen Gulf
Mindoro
Zamboanga
Mindanao
Subic Bay

10/20/1944 ~ Leyte Gulf, Philippines

We left for Leyte Gulf in the Philippines arriving six days later and immediately began firing our 5-inch guns at shore machine gun emplacements   A beachhead 17 miles long was quickly established. when the army hit the beach.

During my Pacific adventures we spent a great deal of time in this country, and I became very familiar with what was happening on a daily basis in this poor little nation. Actually, the people were not really poor because they didn't know any difference and were happy with their way of life.

As you know, I have not been trying to write a historical review. I have been trying to give you a picture of what was happening to a young (eighteen/twenty year old) sailor who was caught up in the middle of a complete disaster. I'm not sure what the heck we Americans were doing in the Philippines in the first place. I am sure we offered the people protection from aggressors and you can be sure they were wondering who was going to protect them from us. One thing for sure, we did not stop the Japanese from taking over the country in a matter of hours and shed a lot of blood taking it back.

I have nothing but the fondest memories of the people as a whole. They were very friendly and made you feel welcome. The place was hot and sticky and everything was dirty, as it's just a way of life. You live in the simplest of terms in a jungle format. Even the cities and villages were years behind the rest of the world but the average person was happy and wanted to be left alone.

When the Japanese bombed Pearl Harbor on December 7th, 1941, The Japan army moved very quickly throughout the Pacific Islands. They didn't make the same mistake as they did in Hawaii. On December 22nd they landed 48 divisions in Lingayen Gulf and 18 divisions just south of Manila

We were totally unprepared. General Wainwright had four infantry divisions and General Moore had one. No one wants to talk about how General MacArthur kept the air force on the ground to be completely destroyed in a matter of hours. The Japanese forces drove our combined armies down into the Bataan Peninsula where they dug in and held out until April 4th Corregidor finally fell on May 1st, 1944.

The major problem that faced a Lieutenant Colonel Tsuji was what to do with 76,000 American and Philippine prisoners of war. The prisoners were starving and sick with malaria, dengue and dysentery and there was no way to house them. Tsuji solved the problem by setting up a ten-day 75-mile march to prison cages in camp San Fernando. When Colonel Tsuji was asked what should be done with all the sick and wounded who were not able to travel, he just pulled out his gun and shot those who were near by. There was no food or medicine so anyone that stopped was shot or bayoneted to death along the trail. Ten thousand died one third Americans and two thirds Filipino. Think about it, pick out a place about seventy five miles away and imagine how you would hold up if you had to make this hike. Under those conditions, death would be welcome.

Shortly before the fall of Corregidor the cryptologists who had our codes committed to memory were removed from the islands by submarine and General MacArthur put his family on PT Boats and headed for Australia.

Except for the Islands of Hawaii, Midway and New Guinea, the Japanese made a clean sweep of the Pacific. During the next year, our country was taking a beating on all fronts. Finally we were able to get our act together and started a new counter offensive in the first months of 1943. Our industrial might and mobilization of manpower began to rise up just as General Yamamoto had predicted on December 7, 1941. He had said that their action at Pearl Harbor "Would awaken a sleeping giant", and with the assistance of Seaman Milton Rhea (I'm sure it was me he was talking about?) things took a turn toward an American victory.

Now Hear This ~ Oh no, not again ?

I remember very clearly the time in the Leyte Gulf that things got very quiet at a meeting in my little boat. I knew something big was going on and I sure didn't like what I was hearing, It sounded like another Pearl Harbor was in the making and we were right in the middle of it with nowhere to run and hide.

Somebody named John Paul Jones once said ~"We have not yet begun to fight", he didn't ask me or I would have said, "Man, - I'm out of here" !

"Now hear this" ~ Read this, It's important

The following was taken from the Rock Mount's reunion bulletin.

The invasion of Leyte Gulf triggers the greatest naval battle of all time. When it was over, the Japanese Navy ceased to exist as an effective fighting force. The incredible heroism by the U.S. Seventh Fleet Officers and men on little escort carriers and thin-skinned destroyers stopped a powerful enemy fleet from creating havoc with the invasion force making their landings in Leyte Gulf.

The Battle of Leyte Gulf was not a single, grand engagement, but consisted of four major encounters on October 23rd – 25th

that ranged across almost 500,000 square miles of ocean. Some 26 Japanese warships, including three battleships, four aircraft carriers and two cruisers were sunk. American losses were three destroyers, two escort carriers and a light cruiser.

When it became apparent that Leyte was to be invaded, the Japanese warlords activated the SHO (Victory Plan). It called for the Combined Fleet (everything they had) to sally forth and annihilate the Americans, both at sea and land in the Leyte Gulf.

Another integral part of SHO is the willingness to sacrifice aircraft carriers to lure Admiral Halsey's Third Fleet away from guarding the entrances to Leyte Gulf. The "bait" for Halsey was four aircraft carriers and two battleship carriers. The latter are hybrids, with a flight deck running out behind

the forward superstructure of a battleship. Vice Admiral
Jisaburo Osawa commanded this fleet; which was waiting to
be spotted about 500 miles north of Leyte.

GAMBIER BAY and other ships of "Taffy 3," aided by planes of "Taffy 2"
had stopped the powerful Japanese Center Force and inflicted a great
loss. Two enemy cruisers were sunk and much damage inflicted on the
other ships of this overwhelmingly powerful surface fleet, turned back
in the last analysis by the indomitable spirit of the men of the escort
carriers and their screen of destroyers and destroyer-escorts.

GAMBIER BAY received four battle stars for service in World War II and
shared in the award of the Presidential Unit Citation to "Taffy 3" for
extraordinary heroism in the battle off Samar.

Admiral Taekko Kurita's powerful center attack force sailed from Brunei Bay, Borneo with 15 destroyers, 12 cruisers and 15 battleships, including the world's largest fighting ships, the Musahi and the Yamato (68,000 ton monsters each with nine 18 inch guns). His plan was to attack through San Bernardino Strait, which separates Luzon and Samar, Leyte. Another Japanese task force with two battleships, three heavy cruisers, a light cruiser, and 11 destroyers tried to force its way through the Surigao Strait south of Leyte and trap the Americans in a giant pincers movement.

Kurita's main force is spotted in the early hours of October 23rd by the U.S. submarines, Darter and Dace. The darter slams two torpedoes into the heavy cruiser Agato. Kurita's flagship, which sinks leaving the admiral struggling in the water. He is finally hauled aboard the Yamato.

In bang, bang fashion the Darter hits the Takeo with two "fish" knocking the heavy cruiser out of action and Dace's four torpedoes slam into the cruiser Maya, which disappears, in an enormous explosion.

Halsey's carrier planes sight Kurita's attack force on the morning of October 24th in the Sibuyan Sea, west of San Bernardino Strait. As Halsey orders his fighters and bombers to strike the enemy, Japanese Navy planes based on Luzon wing on toward the American carriers.

The light carrier Princeton was hit with a 550-pound bomb that hurtled through three decks and starts a gasoline fire. Almost six hours later, there is a huge explosion in the ship's torpedo storage room. Steel debris rained down on the light cruiser, Birmingham, which was along side her decks crowded with men. The carnage was hideous. The Birmingham backs off with 229 of her crew dead and 420 wounded. The Princeton is scuttled.

Halsey's pilots riddle the battleship, Mausahi, with 19 torpedoes and 17 bomb hits. She finally rolled over and sinks, taking 39 officers and 984 men with her. The heavy cruiser Myoko is crippled and retires from battle. Kurita's battered fleet reversed course at 3:00 p.m. to seek respite from incessant air attacks. Halsey is led to believe by his excited airman that Kurita is retreating. He incorrectly assumed that Kurita's force was so badly damaged as to be no of serious threat to those at Leyte Gulf.

Halsey dispatches a battle plan to group commanders at 3:12 p.m. indicating that he will form a task Force 34 to engage the enemy surface forces, consisting of four battleships, two heavy cruisers, three light cruisers, and 14 destroyers.

Halsey's message is also received by all the Pacific Commanders who assumed that he would set up a guard for the San Bernardino Strait against enemy attack. However, at 4:40 p.m. Ozawa's decoy force is sighted and Halsey swallows the bait and sails north taking everything with him. Naval historians will argue this action for decades. Free from attacks for more than an hour and undetected by American reconnaissance, Kurita turned his ships around and steamed east toward the now unguarded San Bernardino

Meanwhile, the southern attack force is sighted plowing toward Surigao Strait on the morning of October 24th. At 1:35
p.m., Kincaid advised his task force to prepare for a night surface attack on Leyte Gulf through Surigao Strait. As the

Japanese ships move single file into the strait, 30 PT boats and a host of destroyers attacked them. Waiting on the eastern side of the strait were the battleships Mississippi, Maryland, West Virginia, Tennessee, California and Pennsylvania.

The six battleships "cross the T" on the Japanese, bringing their broadsides to bear on the enemy column. It is a classic naval tactic dating from the 17th century sailing days. By the time it is over, two enemy battleships, two cruisers and five destroyers are sunk or mortally wounded.

As American seamen were celebrating their victory, all hell breaks loose off Samar, immediately north of Leyte. Kurita's capitol ships went through San Bernardino Strait on the Morning of October 25th and attacked Rear Admiral Clifton Sprague's six escort carriers. Dye marked shells from Japanese battleships and cruisers sent up red, yellow and purple splashes as they straddled the little vessels and hurled fragments onto their decks. A sailor shouts, "My God, they're firing at us in Technicolor".

Sprague launched his planes to attack the enemy dreadnoughts. Fighters and torpedo bombers soared from the flight decks of 12 other little flat tops on station between the onrushing Japanese and Leyte Gulf. Destroyers Johnson, Hoel, and Hermann charged the Japanese ships, firing spreads of torpedoes and hammering enemy decks with 5-inch guns. Riddled by major caliber hits, the burning Hoel sinks at 8:55 a.m. The Johnson, crushed by scores of Japanese shells, goes down an hour later. The destroyer escort, Roberts was ripped apart like a tin can and plunges out of sight.

The slow baby carriers were fishtailing to escape enemy salvos, but the Gambier Bay ran out of luck. Hit, and dead in the water she sinks at 9:00 a.m. Some of her crew were in the water almost 40 hours, fighting sharks. The Gambier Bay is the only U.S. carrier in WWII to be sunk by naval gunfire. Some 115 carrier planes are also lost.

At 11:00 a.m., the baby flat top, St. Lo, was mortally wounded in the first planned kamikaze attack in the war. A Japanese plane smashed through the flight deck and into the bombs and torpedoes stored below. The St. Lo blew up and sank 30 minutes later. As American seamen watched in amazement, Kurita, on the verge of a monumental victory, breaks off all action at 9:11 a.m. and turned his ships north ending the sea battle of Samar.

Naval historians say that the intensity and gallantry of the U.S. aircraft and destroyer attacks led Kurita to believe that he was engaging the big carriers of the Third Fleet and that Halsey's powerful forces were lurking nearby. Kurita's fleet also is badly stung by the swarming Americans. Two cruisers are sunk and a third badly damaged.

Kinkaid's desperate pleas for help and Nimitz's message to Halsey asking, "Where is, repeat, where is task force 34? The whole world wonders". Finally this turned Halsey back south. Halsey was so mad that he threw his hat on the deck and jumped up and down on it.

After the war, Japanese Naval Minister Mitsumasa Yonai said, "Our defeat at Leyte was tantamount to the loss of the Philippines. When you took the Philippines, that was the end of our resources".

Can you imagine how close I came to have "gone swimming"? As I sat aboard the Rocky Mount in the middle of our invasion force in Leyte Gulf, knowing and not being able to say anything to my buddies that if the huge combined Japanese Naval Force would come plowing in the middle of our invasion that was in process, it would have been all over for me, and a few thousand sailors just like me! But fortunately, we were very successful in this huge naval battle and we continued on with the invasion of the Philippines without missing a step.

On October 24th the Rocky Mount sailed for Hollandia, Dutch New Guinea for general drills and then on to the Admiralty and New Guinea Islands for more drills.

October 27th 1944 Another Sea Story about Beer

There were times when our ships would be in an island port waiting for orders to proceed to the invasion. To give the

211

crew a little fun and relaxation, the crew would take our boats ashore to a sandy beach where we could go for a swim, play baseball or just lay around in the very hot sun. Since there was no water on shore, the ships would send in an allotment of four cans of ice cold beer for each sailor. Some how because our ship was a flagship, we were given the best quality beer (Budweiser, Coors, and Millers) where as the other ships got Blue Velvet or some other western beer they really hated.

Being a sweet innocent boy, I didn't like beer anyhow, so I would offer the sailors on the other ships one can of my good beer for two cans of their crummy beer. So I ended up with eight cans of lousy beer. I would swipe some dry ice from the packing cases and keep my beer cold. I would then wait a couple of hours and after everyone had finished drinking their beer and were miserable from the heat and humidity and then I would offer my ice-cold beer to anyone for $5.00 per can. I would take my forty dollars and get into a nickel, dime and quarter poker game and normally lose it all in a short while.

After swimming around for while I would go and stand guard

beside my buddy that ran a dice game. He had an 18x2x4 board and a piece of green felt about two feet square and four pairs of dice. He would smooth out a place on the sand for the felt, and you picked out your dice and tossed them against the board. Someone would place a fifty-dollar bet; my friend would count it and put a rock on the bet. Somebody would cover twenty; some would cover ten and so on until the pot was right. He would count each bet and put the cash between his fingers until the player won or lost and then he would pay off the winners. Any mistakes came out of his pocket. My job was to watch for anyone trying to cheat (which was all the time). What ever the player bet going in was lifted from the total on the third winning roll and given to me. I would put it in a money belt I was wearing. That was the cost of playing in this high roller game. Sometimes there were several hundred bucks involved so this was serious stuff going on here.

By the time we went home he had enough cash saved to buy a new car. He wanted me to spell him once in awhile but I was too chicken. One mistake and you were in big trouble. I had enough trouble with Jap's trying to kill me, and I didn't need a drunken sailor to do it.

December 18th, 1944 ~ Lea, and British New Guinea (My Birthday ~ Would there be any more?)

Most ships went back and fourth to Pearl or San Francisco to be loaded up with supplies and troops. Since our ship was the center of operations, we moved on to the next invasion force heading into Japanese territory. Because of this, our landing craft was constantly on the move picking up supplies from shore or other ships in the area.

It was during some very high seas that one of our boat coxswains got careless on landing and was capsized. The boat was left high and dry on the beach full of sand and water. Our Captain was really bent out of shape. He said we have never lost a boat so go ashore and do whatever is necessary to bring it back. Some of our boat people had a meeting trying to figure out how this could be done and the general consensus was that with the huge waves and the fact that it was about half buried in the sand, it was an impossible task.

Of course, Hollywood (Milt) would come up with the answer. I suggested that we send a crew ashore with shovels and dig a channel from the boat to the water and tie lines to it from a couple of boats and pull out the incapacitated boat through the surf. That seemed logical to me, but they looked at me like I was out of my mind. They asked if I had given any thought to the huge waves crashing on the beach.

I had forgotten that 95% of those guys were from the states that were surrounded by dirt and the idea of getting wet was frightening. I told them those little old waves were just the type that us California body surfers dreamed about. I could easily swim through them with a line tied to my waist that later would be used to haul in heaver lines to tie to the boat.

I knew that I could and could steer the boat through the waves as they pulled it out to a point where we could tie lines from their boats to each side of the "beat up" boat. They said I was crazy, but to go for it

There was a dock about a mile away where they could take a

half dozen guys with shovels ashore. I swam through the surf and pulled in large lines to secure to the boat. While the guys were digging a channel for the boat I took one of the floorboards from the boat and used it as a boogie board to ride the large waves. I was having a ball, but my buddies thought I was crazy. While I was getting my kicks in the breakers, the guys on shore built a large fire to get rid of their chills from the wet sand. This attracted a million mosquitoes so later they all came down with terrible cases of malaria and were sent back to the states with shaking fevers. Since the boat crews were spending time on the shore we were given double shots and it paid off for me. We salvaged the boat and made the Captain happy, but we paid a high price for the effort.

01/05/1945 ~ Luzon and the Lingayen Gulf in the Philippines

The Rock headed north to join and lead an invasion force to Luzon, and the Lingayen Gulf in the Philippines. On the way to Lingayen Gulf and the landing of the 40th U.S. Infantry

Division, some of the action reports filed included: With Rocky Mount as fleet guide, a steering mishap occurred. On a change of course, the wheel went hard right and the rudder went hard left, swinging the bow toward the Mount Olympus, another AGC. The order was given for full speed astern and the Rocky Mount was able to go through the port column between the third and fourth ships. After a few emergency turns, control was shifted back to the bridge. The ship resumed her position as fleet guide. Boy, am I glad I wasn't on the wheel as a helmsman.

January 5th 1945 ~ The Kamikaze

The Kamikaze dive bombers were a divine death wish for Japanese to fight, to die, and join their ancestors in Jap heaven. We fought to live and to join our loved ones at home for a barbeque in the back yard.

Stories about WWII in the Pacific would not be complete with our covering some of the actions of those Japanese pilots that volunteered to become a "Kamikaze". Any man that defends his country has to respect and honor those individuals of the enemy that gave their life for their country. Americans risked their lives, but there was no "risk" for the Kamikaze. It was absolutely final! When you watched them dive to their deaths you couldn't help but say to yourself "COME ON GUYS, THIS AIN'T FAIR, THIS IS NO WAY TO FIGHT A WAR, GIVE ME A BREAK".

Our convoy of ships were stretched from horizon to horizon on the South China Seas, heading north to the Lingayen Gulf in the Philippines. When you looked up into the sky you could see many tiny specks flying around in circles knowing that there were men up there who were going to dive "on your head" in a few minutes. The chill down our backs and lumps in our stomachs was a brand new feeling of terror that we have never experienced before. There was no place to hide. You just stand there and pray that this guy will not choose you for "His emperor's gift".

The ship's loud speaker shouts, "Don't fire until they are with in range of your guns". Everything was very still and time seemed to stop. You have your 20mm gun aimed straight up with the cross hairs of your gun sight right on one of those dots in the sky. Suddenly, down they came and the loud speaker shouts "Commence Firing!". You pull the trigger and you body pulsates with the exploding shells. About every few shells is made of a bright tracer shell so you can see where your shells are going. You try to lead your target and let the plane fly into your line of fire. The whole ship is shaking to the pounding of every gun going off at the same time. You can kiss your eardrums good bye!

The whole sky is full of exploding shells and you know it

would be impossible for anything to fly through the umbrella of exploding shells, but they do; and they just keep coming and coming. You are right on your target and they're getting closer and closer and when they are really low, you realize you are firing into the ship that they are diving into. You stop to watch a huge explosion as the Japanese pilot hits the ship, then its back up into the sky to pick out another plane. The next one gets real close and explodes in the air, and you scream "I got one, I got one!" Of course at the time you're not thinking about all the other guns on all of the other ships aimed at the same planes.

One of the things they don't happen to mention in your training is that everything that goes up must come down. Suddenly you hear the clanging of pieces of shrapnel raining down on the deck around you. I felt a sting down my back, but it was just a scratch but many of my shipmates were seriously wounded. Three of my buddies in the boat crews were hit in the legs with metal the size of a pin head, the doctors left them where they were "no problem" Because they registered in sick buy, later on they were presented with Purple Heart Medals, They were so embarrassed and we kidded the life out of them.

Many times on the television show "Our Nation's History" a Kamikaze was shown diving into the deck of an aircraft carrier with a huge explosion and all the shells going off around it. That ship was just about a half a mile off our starboard side. I still get that sinking feeling in the pit of your stomach when I see it.

Later on, I was down in the stern (back) of the ship for some reason and I climbed up the ladder (stairs), opened the hatch (door), and stepped out on the deck (floor) just as our five-inch gun above me fired. It blew me back through the hatch and down the ladder in a heap on the deck (floor) below. I though that I must be dead, but I was just bruised up a little.

But I had this terrific ringing in my ears, so I proceeded down to sick bay. The doctor said it would go away in a few days – and it did.

Recently I went to an audiologist and purchased some hearing aids and when he looked at the results of my test he said, "Oh, we have a Navy WW2 gunner here, right?" I said,

"I guess you know one when you hear one".

01/06/1945

An emergency turn was executed to avoid a reported submarine contact ahead. The destroyer Suesens dropped depth charges.

01/08/1945 ~ An enemy plane approached from the starboard quarter and crashed into the carrier Kitkum Bay about 5,000 yards away. She had to be taken under tow by a fleet tug.

I SAW IT, I SAW IT, I SAW IT, ~ The other night on the History Channel, I noticed that a camera man showed a picture of my boat pulling away from our ships gang way. Because of the configuration of my boat was different from any other boat with two twenty millimeter machine guns in front of the cabin, I'm sure that it was mine. You couldn't see me because I was in the cabin. What a kick.

01/09/1945

A Japanese Zero came to the Rock's starboard quarter at an altitude of 2,000 yards. In 30 seconds 650 rounds of 20-millimeter, 122 rounds of 20-millimeter, and 10 rounds of 5-inch shells were expended. The enemy aircraft was seen to crash on the beach about a minute later.

01/09/1945 ~ The Lingayen Gulf

Our huge convoy made it's way through the Philippine Islands and the China Seas to the mainland of Luzon and it's very large Lingayen Gulf. I understand that every ship dropped anchor within fifty feet of the ship's destination. The Rocky Mount was the lead ship and it's twenty-five year old navigator led the way for everyone.

There was very little resistance on the beaches, so our main force assembled quickly and spread out across Luzon. This is ugly country with muddy beaches, thick jungle and little villages with muddy streets. General Mac Arthur wanted to capture the capital city of Manila and it's 800,000 people by his 65th birthday so that he could ride in a parade in his honor

The Japanese were really dug in and hundreds of troops were lost. He also had all of the small islands to the south cleared of enemy soldiers with heavy loss of life. All of this was unnecessary. They were in a helpless position but this was a personal vendetta to prove how wonderful he was.

The Japanese still had one more trick up their sleeve. They built small boats with a powerful engine and loaded the front half with explosives. It could be hidden in the bushes. When the time was right they would come flying out, and drive directly into the mid ship of an anchored ship blowing a hole about fifteen feet in circumference. Of course the driver and the boat was never to be seen again; and even if the ship did not sink, it was out of business.

We stationed a man at the bow, one on each side mid ship and one on the stern, each with a rifel. We also stationed one of our landing craft about a hundred feet away going around and around the ship all day and night with machine guns. Shooting a Thomson Machine gun is a real kick. It's almost impossible hit anything with it, it's all you can do to just hold it in your hands but you do cover a large area with hits Once again, I believed that our ship's camouflage confused the Japanese because they left us alone. I saw on television the other night that the Japanese were producing hundreds of these boats to protect their mainland when and if we invaded their shores.

Occasionally a Kamikaze would fly in out of the blue, but for the most part it was very quiet so I looked for something to do. Admiral Royal didn't go for meetings in our boat. I drove a landing craft up one of the rivers until I came to this little town that had many little houses built out over water. I started up a conversation with a young man (they all looked like either kids or a hundred years old) who was fishing and I asked him how was it under Japanese occupation. He replied it was just fine, they were nice people except they would stand around until he caught a fish, then they would take it and cut the head off and eat it, and he said they all smelled bad. I asked him about Americans and he said we were nice too, but sometimes they had to keep their women inside their houses if the men in brown uniforms were around.

He was really proud to be able to speak a little English. He had gone to a missionary school at one time. He wanted to show us (the three of us) his new home he had just built so we went to his house which was made of bamboo tied very tightly together with Palm branches for the roof. He had a big clay pot in the corner for an open fire cook stove. His sweet little wife insisted that we eat some fried rice and boiled eggs. We sat and played with their two little kids. For sailors who were a million miles from home this was really fun. He wanted to talk about America and it was next to impossible because he didn't have a clue as to our life style and how we lived. It got so late that he gave us some mats and we slept on his little porch over the water. The next morning, his wife almost cried because they didn't really have food for us. We had eaten up all of their food the night before. You talk about three stupid and embarrassed sailors.

When we went back to the boat we walked through an area covered with woven mats. When one of the mats moved I looked closely and found there was a little old person sleeping in each woven mat bag. A kind of old folks Sun City home.

I promised that we would be back so the little wife made me print my name on a piece of paper. A couple of days later we went back to see them and she gave me a small handkerchief made of parachute rayon with my name embroidered on it. She said she takes old clothes apart for the thread. They were completely shocked when we gave them three cases of canned goods we had swiped from the galley aboard ship. These were really sweet innocent people.

One of our boat crews found an abandoned small submarine run up on the beach. They went inside and found several cases of Sake. I was afraid to drink it but these guys from the Virginia back woods will drink anything that has alcohol in it. We claimed we had captured it under heavy machine gun fire, but nobody would buy our story.

We had a real old guy about forty aboard ship that would buy up all the Aqua Green Velvet shaving lotion and lock it up in his locker. He kept it for when he would get the shakes. I would hear him getting up in the middle of the night to take a drink (sad).

The Islands of Iwo Jima and Okinawa

February 19th,1945 ~ The invasions of Iwo Jima and Okinawa
Invasions. I was fortunate to miss because I was in a different part of the Pacific. About this time the old "Rock" was on its way from Lingayen Gulf to Subic Bay in the Philippines. I felt that since they were the bloodiest battles to date, I should include them in my sea stories to remain objective in the over all trail of American blood to Tokyo. I understood that my old Admiral (Bloody Kelly) Turner and General Howlin Mad Smith was spear heading the troops "Why am I not surprised?" It was of general opinion that we needed these islands to be able to supply the B29s with fighter protection during the invasion of Japan. As it turned out the atomic bomb convinced the Japanese to finally raise the white flag of surrender so both of the invasions of Iwo Jima and Okinawa in June were academic. This is easy to say, but when you look at the statistics one wonders who the

hell was running our war department. Iwo Jima was five miles long and two and one half miles wide, 625 miles south to Siapan and 660 miles north to Tokyo. With miles of underground tunnels and lines of bunkers. Twenty-one thousand Japanese were killed with 1,000 prisoners. We sent 880 ships with 74,000 Marines and 110,000 soldiers. Six thousand of our troops were killed and 18,000 were wounded with 500 missing in action. Okinawa was the most horrible operation of the war (larger than Normandy). We had 70,000 casualties with 12,000 of our troops killed. The Japanese lost 100,000 dead (hard to believe). Why did we need to take both islands? As a matter of fact, with all of our new aircraft carriers, why did we bother with the Philippians? By this time, we had practically destroyed their Navy, their pilots and planes were mostly gone. They didn't have anything left to fight with. But after all, we had all those troops and equipment so we might as well use them! Right!?

During these operations Admiral Halsey took a fleet through a monster storm. He could have gone around the storm but living up to his repartition he went right in to it. We lost two large destroyers and all of their crews. It was later found to

229

be completely his fault but nothing was done to this great officer.

02/29/1945 ~ The Island of Zamboanga

We sailed to Subic Bay, Mindoro Island and Leyte Gulf gathering up Australians to make up an attack force of an assault on the islands of Zamboanga and Mindanao in the Philippines. This operation took about two weeks to blow away the shore batteries and establish a secure beachhead. They say that the monkeys have no tails but you can't prove it by me ? We then sailed back to the Leyte Gulf, Philippines...

Oh, you look so sweet coming down the street (passageway)

I remember one time when I was working with the deck painting crew; I developed a friendship with a fellow that was sort of "different". This tall, skinny kid seemed to enjoy the painting that was going on continuously aboard the ship. He would take a large piece of cardboard, paint it white, and then dip his fingers into the paints that we were using, and then paint pictures of the ships and islands that were near by. He didn't have much choice when it came to color, but he blended them into really great paintings. One day, I asked him to show me how to paint, and he said "okay". He showed me how to draw a person's right eye. The problem was that he never got around to showing me how to draw the left eye. I can draw a whole face ~ but the left eye, to this day, never looks right at me. He had one little problem that doesn't work on a ship full of rugged sailors. When he talked he sounded like a sweet little girl. We all referred to him as "Mary". One day I asked him if he was a "fairy". He said, "Hell no! When I joined the Navy, I was sleeping with three different women ~ whichever was available". He said that his parents were wealthy and both of them were famous artists in New York, and in the crowd he grew up with, everyone talked "that way". One day, a tough "old hillbilly" grabbed him and pushed him into the paint locker. My buddy, "Mary" pulled out a bayonet from his tool box, and chased this jerk all over the ship. That put an end to the wise-cracking about my friend, "Mary"!

Draw one ~ you lose.

Everybody played poker all the time. It was just a way of life.

One time - after a couple of years in the Navy, I received a report on how much I had earned to date. We didn't make much money, but I was amazed at how much money I had earned to date and the only money I could remember spending was buying a lovely wrist watch for my Mother in Hawaii. I was broke ~ as usual, and it didn't make any sense ~ that is until I realized I had been playing nickel, dime and quarter poker every day and night since coming aboard ship! So, I QUIT - cold turkey! I started playing double deck pinochle and found a friend that taught me how to play chess. I got to be very good at both of them, and, of course, I had my little business of selling beach souvenirs that I had picked on shore to the crew. I was amazed at how "rich" I was when I got home. We had a bunch of guys that played poker for high stakes. They had a game going 24 hours a day. A couple of my shipmates would actually cry when we would refuse to lend them more money to play. They had one very interesting rule, and that was that it was perfectly all right to cheat, peek, and mark or "palm" the high cards. In fact, anything you wanted to do to win! If they caught you, you had to sit out that hand and lose everything you had in the "pot". No one would get mad - or get killed, but it was just part of the challenge to play with the big money "pros". This was one place that was "out of bounds for me".

The President's Memorial

We then sailed to Morotai Island where all hands attended a memorial service on the fantail of our ship for the President. It was too bad he didn't see the end of the war that he devoted his life to. He made some terrible mistakes at Potsdam and about not warning the Admiral in Hawaii on December 6th and his support of General MacArthur when other leaders in the pacific were so much more deserving, but through out all of his time in office he did wonders for our country.

The Island of Borneo
Brunei Bay
Tarakan

04/23/1945 ~ The invasion of Tarakan, Borneo

After assembling the Australians we departed for an assault landing on Tarakan Island at Borneo. The troops and all of their weapons were loaded on our LSTs landing craft and we were on our way. On of my barbershop quartet buddies, Nate Humlet was a skipper on one of these tubs They were so slow you would spit in the ocean and watch the bubble go by, but of course we had to stay with these big old barges. We were sitting ducks for any submarines lurking nearby. We were really concerned.

When a large ammunition dump blew up nearby, The explosion was so intense we thought we were in big trouble. When something like this happens there is a period of confusion until you figure out what really happened. We anchored in the mouth of a large river and the tide was so fast that the LSTs were sitting on the bottom at low tide. I had to go full speed in my boat to stay even with my ship at anchor. There was very little resistance to our Navy so we returned to Morotai for a brief rest and preparation for our next invasion. (It never seemed to stop.)

06/03/1945 ~ Brunei Bay, Borneo

We established a beachhead quickly. Those Aussies were really tough and rugged guys. The jungle was so thick you could only see a couple of feet through the green vines. It was so hot and the humidity was worse than any of our other adventures.

I think by now you have got the idea that I was not one to follow orders all of the time, some times you just had to be a little creative and do your own thing.

I remember doing a little sight seeing one day at a very small island off shore from the mainland. We anchored our boat and swam ashore and hiked up to the top of a rise in the middle of the island to look around. To our surprise there were several rubber boats with the Aussies making a full-scale invasion on the other side. At first we thought it would be fun to go down and welcome them to our paradise, or to get off of our island! but then they started shooting at something so we decided we had better get the hell off that island, now. We ran as fast as we could through the jungle and I ran into a large swarm of flying red ants. Those babies don't just sting, they bite pieces of flesh away. They followed me right into the ocean and I rubbed them off under water.

Never volunteer ~ I knew that ?

Someone asked me to volunteer for some activity on the beach and as usual being bored to death, I said sure why not. It seems that one of our pilots found a Japanese prison camp a few miles back from shore and saw some white prisoners behind the fence. He said there was a large river flowing by the camp, but that it disappeared into the jungle overgrowth. So we took a landing craft with five men with machine guns and a navigator with a compass. We went down the coast until we found the river coming out of the jungle. Then we would go up the river as far as we could or until the river became a swamp. We would go back down the coast until we found another river and would go through the same process. We did this over and over until we found a river that didn't get smaller and was headed for that prison camp. We also spotted basketball size mines floating just under the surface at the mouth of the river. We made this executive decision that this project was too big for us little guys and we should get the hell out of there. You have to get the picture here. The jungle was so thick you couldn't see five feet into the vines. Most of the time the growth covered over the river so you were in sort of a dark cave and you knew that around every bend there would be a bunch of Jap's waiting to blow you away. Also the heat and humidity was so hot and thick we were soaking wet from head to toe. I'm telling you, this was scary stuff! When we got back to the ship, we suggested they send a bunch of Australian commandos up the river in very quiet rubber boats. This was done, but I never heard what the results were.

Borneo is the armpit of the world. Don't go there, ever. The only good thing about Borneo was that if I hadn't been there I would have been at Iwo Jima and Okinawa Islands, and I wouldn't be writing these dumb little sea stories

Letters, More precious than gold

My sweet darling mother kept a solid stream of letters coming to me regardless of all of her problems at home, and she had plenty of difficult times to deal with. I could always look forward to a stack of letters at mail call. Sometimes it would be several weeks before our mail caught up with us.

Since I joined the Navy during high school, I had a whole bunch of girl friends that made it their duty to write constantly. They all went to our local Hollywood photographers and had pictures taken to make them look like movie stars. I hardly recognized them. I stuck their pictures up on the inside of my locker door, and of course, I would leave the door ajar to make sure my shipmates could sneak a peek at them. My brother was an extra at several Hollywood studios, and I would point him out in some of the backgrounds of the old "B" movies we were shown to the troops. My friends were very "impressed", and consequently I was given the nickname "Hollywood". The guys were sure I was part of the glamour scene (and that was my joke)! I was really pleased that I didn't have a deep commitment to any of those girls because of the pain I saw among the married shipmates around me. They missed their loved ones so passionately it was all they could think or talk about. We were gone so very long that the inevitable finally started happening. We called them "Dear John letters". They all basically said the same thing (how lonely they were and how they had made friends with this wonderful guy at work, and now they had fallen in love and have decided to get married, "So will you please sign the enclosed divorce papers"). Some were afraid to open their mail. I don't think any of these girls had the slightest idea how this destroyed those poor guys! To be wounded and die on the battlefield would have been preferable for some of them.

Above, I said that I was glad I had no commitments, but that's not really true. I learned how wonderful it would have been to have a true and meaningful relationship, to love and be loved by a caring woman, and how fragile this love can be.

After leaving the service and dating several girls for a couple of years, I decided that there was no such thing as the perfect one for me, and then "Wham ~ Bang ~Alacazamm This wonderful red head named Ruby came into my life and I was captured, no, I mean I've been captivated since 1948.

She presented me with two fantastic sons, our first born, Randy, was lost serving as a Green Beret on a hilltop in Vietnam.

One of the most painful experiences that can happen to a father is to greet a young soldier early on a Sunday morning at your door that tells you he has a message from our President who would like you to know that your wonderful son has giving his life for his country. And then you have to some how inform his poor mother and younger brother. Talk about pain! Have you ever rolled up in a ball on your kitchen floor and gasping for air?

One of the most difficult part of writing this book is being reminded that the parents of all of those thousand of boys lost had to go through the same experience as I did.

Our other son, Darrel, his wonderful wife and his two boys, Randy W. and Casey will carry on our legacy and make us proud and complete.

June 18th 1945 ~ Admiral Forrest Royal Died

Our Rear Admiral Forrest B. Royal was found dead in his cabin. He died of a heart attack during the night. He was about fifty pounds overweight. We held a memorial service for him the next day aboard ship. They stored his body in our meat locker until we reached port. (Nobody wanted meat for dinner!!)

06/23/1945 ~ Preparations for the Invasion of Japan

The Rocky Mount was tied up to the repair ship Vulcan for an overhaul and preparing our ship for the mother of all invasions, Japan. There were hundreds of ships in the Leyte Gulf waiting for that hellish day.

 I ran an air line over to our ship and hooked up a paint sprayer for my crew (I was in charge of the top two decks and the smokestack at this time). We did a fast job of finishing all our paint areas in just a few hours. When we were standing back admiring our beautiful work, the Captain came by and wanted to know who painted everything. He said "Don't you know the regulations say that you have to paint by hand with a brush". I told him we had just completed three days work in one so what's the problem? He said "OK wise guy, you tell me what are you going to do with your crew for the next two days." I told him I thought it would be nice if we went to the beach for a swim. He said "How long do you plan on being in this mans Navy?" I said that the day this war is over, I'm going straight home. He smiled and said "Thank God" and walked off.

These weeks of waiting for the Japanese invasion, our great leaders put together all sorts of sports programs, aboard ship and on shore. I remember we had to stop a baseball game to allow pictures to be taken of General MacArthur stepping out of a landing craft into a couple of feet of water on the beach. We laughed and yelled, "I will return". In all of the Admiral's and General's discussions and planning, I never overheard General Macarthur's name mentioned once. I thought that he was the presidents PR man.

One of my "good buddies" in the boat crews signed me up to be a light heavy weight fighter, They thought that this was really funny so to save face I just had to do it. I had never had a fistfight in my life. One of the guys in our boat crews had been a fighter before the service. He had a flat nose, glassy eyes. Since he fought middleweight level I asked him to train me so every day for about an hour he beat the heck out of me. He was really fast. About the time I began to think

I was pretty tough, a black guy from the repair ship next to us came over and asked if I would work out with him. When he took off his shirt, I knew I was in big trouble. He looked like a weight lifter and said he was the champion of the 11 Naval District. (That's the state of California) We started boxing and I hit him with some pretty good shots and then he hit me in the face with a couple of straight jabs and my nose exploded, then a right to my solar plexus and I could no longer breath and then he hit me with a left hook and I was sure my head had left my body and was rolling on the deck. I felt like all I really wanted to do was go to take a nap. I finally stopped him and told him I had this problem of feeling faint at the sight of my own blood and he should find someone else to destroy.

When it was fight time, I think the odds were a hundred to one in favor of this big Pollock from the coal mines. But much to my surprise and everyone else, he was so slow I beat him up easily. I lost my next fight on points so I learned the agony of defeat. My next fight was scheduled with a guy that had knocked out all of his opponents in the first round of every fight. After giving this some real thought I said "OK" I quit. They can keep there lousy $25.00 war bond first prize.

My teeth were crooked but they were all I had. I proved that in this war a smart coward could live another day!!! My buddies gave me a bad time but I think they respected me for at least making an effort to get involved.

I played on our ships basket ball team when our ship played a team on an aircraft carrier on an interior deck. They play all of the time so they made us look like clods. We had a baseball team that played on shore. After floating around for years, this was really fun.

August 10th 1945 @ 2100 – O'clock
Do you remember what you were doing at that time? (Maybe you weren't born yet)

I heard there was going to be a USO show that night on a ship nearby, so a couple of us borrowed a boat and quietly made our way over to this ship. Sure enough there was a full band and a bombshell actress, Betty Hutton, singing like crazy along with some show girls dancing. We tied up to the stern and went aboard. About the time we were engrossed in the show, a nearby ship started blowing its foghorn. We were bent out of shape because we couldn't hear the girls. About that time another ship started blowing it's foghorn and then another and another, and then people were firing the pyrotechnics out of life boats up in the air. As all of the sailors started cheering, we looked at each other and said My God, this it can't be true? But it was, and I we were still alive. Ill be darned, we can't quit now, We haven't invaded Japan yet Someone said that we dropped a really big bomb and blew away half of the country. I did not have any problems with that at all. I immediately went looking for those show girls but they were all up in the officers quarters celebrating and drinking what looked like campaign. I was told I was out of bounds and asked in an very official way to get the hell out of there. O well it was worth a try.

In retrospect, Today, I wonder if we really needed to drop something as horrible as the atomic bomb. We were fire bombing there factories to a point that Japan was really out of business. There Navy and Air force was gone and we were in complete charge. It was just a matter of time, Hind sight is all ways perfect.

Yo, Ho, Ho and a bottle of Rum ~ What do I care ~ I'm going home.

The Rocky Mount was detached from Commander Seventh Fleet Amphibious Force and reported to the Pacific Fleet. We proceeded to Manila to bring aboard Admiral Thomas C. Kinkaid, as he was to sail to the Yangtze River in China. It was decided that a few of the crew could be transferred ashore to be sent home, so they held a lottery to see who would be lucky enough to go first. All of the crew aboard was on the Rocky Mount since it was commissioned. So I reminded the officer in charge (with a very intense attitude) that I was transferred aboard by Admiral Turner in the Marshall Islands; that I had already been through the Battle of the Gilbert Islands on the USS Pierce before the Rocky Mount left Hoboken. And furthermore, I had more points than any one on the ship! So after me, they could have their damned lottery. I don't think he liked the look in my eyes, so he agreed.

After listening to some of my shipmates stories at our reunions, I should have gone on to China with the ship. They had some fantastic experiences that I missed out on but at that time in history all I could think of was going home.

Manila Harbor was a real mess with several ships sitting on the bottom with their superstructure sticking out of the water. The city was pretty well shot up as well. So they trucked us to the outskirts of town to a tent city for GI's going home. I had to stay there for about two weeks before an old liberty freighter was found for me to board. I wasn't sure it could make it across the Pacific, but I would swim if I had to, and I think I could have swam faster than that old liberty ship could go! But, as long as I was heading east, I didn't care about anything! We had to take salt water showers with big bars of hard yellow soap. I found a steam pipe that I was able to put a can of drinking water on to heat up to shave with.

After about a week, one night someone started yelling that he thought he saw a light, so everyone went topside. Sure enough, right out there on the horizon was a beautiful bright light and the next thing we knew we were cold, I hadn't been cold for almost three years and it felt so good! About six o'clock that morning, we entered the mouth of the Straits of

San Juan de Fuca in Washington. It was cold and drizzly, but out of the fog came a tugboat. There must have been twenty young girls on this little boat, waving and cheering! These kids were the first white girls that I had looked at in almost three years. We all started yelling and as we ran over to the side rail to see them, the ship heeled over so far that our Captain was screaming for us to get back to mid-ship. The tug went around and around the ship and I thought we were going to flip over each time. What a nice thing for those girls to do.

In Seattle we finally tied up to the dock about noon and you could see office buildings, drug stores, used car lots, streets, sidewalks, and real people all dressed up very nice. It was wonderful! You can't believe how mind blowing it was.

We were bussed to a naval base (I forget which one), and issued some fresh Navy clothes. Then we went through the chow line and I almost cried for joy! There was fried chicken, fresh vegetables and Milk "Honest to God" real milk
I drank two glasses before I left the chow line. We then went to the showers. I remember lying on the floor with the water

as hot as I could stand it pouring down on me for what seemed like hours.

The sailors on the base were so kind to us. I hadn't had a haircut in months. I had two very painful boils as big as fifty cent pieces, one on my elbow and another on the back of my neck. The China crud left sores all over by body so I guess I was a sad sight to see. It was amazing how fast my body healed with good food and some rest. But everything was OK, As every day was a thrilling thing to behold. I went to downtown Seattle and ate in restaurants, went to theaters and looked at the girls. Wow, Seattle was having a heat spell and all the men were in short sleeve sport shirts. I wore my sweater, pea coat and a heavy wool watch cap pulled down over my ears, as my blood was as thin as water – and I was still cold!

Hi Mom, Hi Dad, Hi big Brother

I was issued orders to Terminal Island in Long Beach, California along with a train ticket to Los Angeles and a thirty-day leave. Upon arriving in L.A. I caught a bus for Beverly

Hills where my mother worked as a telephone operator for the Robinsons Department Store. I took an elevator up to the top floor and asked a lady to find Mrs. Rhea and tell her that a sailor is out here looking for a date for lunch. She laughed and disappeared through a door. In a moment I heard seven telephone operators screaming with joy! The door flew open and Mom came running out with tears flowing down her cheeks. After we hugged for a long time, she pulled me by the arm into the telephone office. They were all crying, and I had to hug every one of them. For almost three years they had listened to my mother crying every time there was another invasion in the Pacific. Needless-to-say, it was quite awhile before anyone made any telephone calls to or from that department store.

It was so good to hold my dad again. He never made waves or was very emotional about what was going on around him, but quietly went about his life making the best of things. My mother admitted to me that the biggest mistake she ever made in her life was leaving him. Earning a lot of money was not one of his talents, but I never knew a person that knew him that didn't love him, and I am proud to be his son.

I was pleasantly surprised to learn that I had a real "honest to goodness" brother and a beautiful blond sister in law, Bunny. I was now twenty years old (almost twenty-one) and Freddy was twenty-nine. The nine years between us seemed to disappear in a minute. Freddy, being a professional musician and comedian made the miserable life we had before the war seemed like a joke, and I never laughed so hard in all my life! (I was ready for a good laugh.)

My brother, Freddy, had an orchestra at the Beverly Hills Hotel and his day job was working as a part-time actor at the studios. He felt it was his responsibility to see that there were plenty of lovely starlets to keep his little brother busy during my thirty-day leave. He also explained that I was home now and people didn't use profanity with every other word like sailors do aboard ship in the middle of the Pacific.

He set me up so that whenever I would take a date to the Beverly Hills Hotel nightclub (where he was playing), everyone including the doorman and headwaiter would treat me like I was a visiting sultan, giving me the best table and

251

make over me. Freddy would approach us and ask if there was something the lady would like the orchestra to play for her. The poor girl would look at me with big eyes in wonder, and it was all I could do to keep a straight face. I got a lot of mileage out of that scenario.

When I checked in at the Terminal Island Navy Base, I was so exhausted, I didn't wake up for two days, but I sure had a great thirty-day leave! Later on, Ruby never forgave me for spending all of my "accumulated wealth" from my sailor pay before we met.

December 15th 1945 ~ Medals of Valor

The four medals and the six bronze stars presented to me by the U.S. Navy were not something that I have considered very exciting because everyone around me aboard ship received the same honor, so it was no big deal.

The blue ribbon was for serving in the Pacific. The gold ribbon was for serving in the South Pacific. The red ribbon was for serving with the invasion forces in the Philippine

Liberation, and the green ribbon was for those who were on the USS Rocky Mount during the many times we were under intense battle conditions. The six bronze stars were for personal involvement.

Now that I look back on the whole war, I can see now that it was a big deal – A great big deal Just being out there in the middle of the ocean with all of the action going on around me was a big deal.   Then there were the constant attacks by the submarines and aircraft that either sunk or damaged our ships severely every day.

At the time, we didn't think much about it because it just came
with the territory. You certainly didn't choose to be there, but since you were there, you did what had to be done. Well, it wasn't quite that simple. When you laid in your bunk at night and listened to the waves slapping the side of the ship which was only a couple of inches thick (built by the lowest bidder) you were wondering how long the seams would hold together. Then there were all of those sharks swimming around out there!

One time I woke up in the middle of the night and found myself standing out on the deck in my shorts! When I went back to bed, one of my buddies told me that a big wave slapped the ship's side, and I flew out of there! Is there a Japanese submarine out there a few hundred yards away with your ship in the cross hairs of it's periscope? Will I live another day? Everyone has a day like that once in a while, but how about maybe 700 days like that in a row? War is Hell As I have said before in this little book, when I sat in the theater and saw the opening scenes of the movie "Saving Private Ryan", the physical and mental pain floating around in my subconscious came bursting forth and I really frightened myself. I lost control of my emotions, and shook and cried like a baby. After sixty years, that's unbelievable!

These Medals are a Big Deal

When I look at all of my son's medals on the wall, I am reminded once again of the ultimate sacrifice he made for our country; and the medals that represent the thanks our nation has tried to show.

It's Somebody Else's Problem

This little addition does not have any historical value except t
that at the time it was foremost on my mind. While I was
waiting around at the Terminal Island Navy Base to be
discharged, one day I heard my name being called out over
the public address system to report to draft number 1221
being assembled to proceed to Hawaii to relieve sailors
coming home for discharge.

Needless-to-say, this got my full attention. When I talked to
the Yeoman (head bookkeeper) in charge he said he didn't
know anything about it, but that my name was on the list to go
and "that was that, so report for duty". I kept my cool and
Explained in a quiet voice that I also was waiting for
discharge
and had all of the points necessary so there had to be some
sort of mistake.
If they sent me over to Hawaii, they would have to send me
back again, and that would delay my discharge for several
weeks.
He explained that it was too late to make any changes in the

orders and he was very sorry. I told him to look me in the eyes because I wanted to be sure he understood what my position was. I had just returned from spending almost three years of continuous sea duty with no liberty and had made shore landings on six separate bloody invasions killing people for my government, and I could assure him I was not going to go back overseas. The way I looked at it, he could change my orders or he would end up with at least one broken arm and I wasn't sure what else.

He told me that after giving the whole thing some serious thought, he could see I wasn't being treated fairly and I was not to say anything to anybody. When it was time for the draft to leave, my name would not be on the list. I was to be quiet and just wait until my name was called for a formal discharge.

Sure enough, I watched my draft of about a hundred men get on trucks and disappear toward the shipyards. Every few days I would drop by his office and smile at him and he would smile back. After a couple of weeks my name was called, and I was officially discharged with about fifty other sailors. I proved I had learned that there was the correct way or the

Navy way to get things done. You just keep smiling.

YO, HO, HO and they can keep their dammed bottle of rum,
 I ain't no sailor no mo, no mo

I was discharged the first week of January. I've forgotten the
exact date, but it was a great day.

Attention Sailor, Salute me, eyes straight ahead, "or else""

That's Tradition and That's Power ~ There is one thIng
that bugged me during my Navy days. I would like to write
about the cohabitation of officers and enlisted men and why I
couldn't wait to get out of the Navy due to their non-
fraternization policy that really rubbed my integrity the wrong
way.

Navy tradition has it that officers are very intelligent gentlemen and enlisted men are a whole lot less, I mean a whole lot less. I was close to many officers that I learned to respect and I believe they respected me. I would have enjoyed their company on a personal basis, but this was impossible because of Navy tradition.

Really, if an officer wanted to say a few friendly words to me, he would look around to make sure no one was watching because he could get in trouble with his superiors. (This was not true with the Admirals.)

On the other hand, I met many men who happen to have two years of junior college and 90 days in officers training school and because of their lack of experience and intelligence they tried to cover their ineptness' up by being overly demanding and showing a whole lot of disrespect to the enlisted men around him. Of course this was perfectly acceptable because of Navy tradition. This was a major problem then and is today as well. Some would say that in order to be in command of a person of a lesser rank, there has to be a separation of personal position and I am in complete disagreement. (I know I've lost this battle before I start). During my forty years as a some what of a successful business operator and owner, I have always considered my employees to be on an equal basis to myself and they were rewarded by their ability to produce. This had everything to do with success of our production and morale within our company and anything to the contrary is just plain ridiculous.

He who has the big guns ~ Wins

Since this a collection of stories is about my own personal experience, I may seem to skip over important factors in the overall fighting that was occurring most of the time. One of these elements was the activity of the major Battleships, Aircraft Carriers, Cruisers and of course, the many Destroyers
during the whole conflict.

Those of us who were cruising along in our "fat little ships" full of soldiers and marines in huge convoys on our way to invasions, really felt confident when we looked out to sea and there were battleships, cruisers, aircraft carriers and destroyers and far as the eye could see in all directions. We knew they were there, but our thoughts were almost totally involved with what we were about to encounter on the beaches ahead, skies above and below the surface. One of the things that went through our minds was that all of these sailors who have come all of the way over here, and all they did was sit and watch our smoke and fire on the beach. There were several major battles in the Solomon Islands (called the slot). Coral Sea, Philippines and Midway Island between the Japanese combined fleet and our far flung "power house floating cities". The battles that were going on at sea were brutal, but we didn't see them. They were just over the horizon, and we were happy about that. On the morning of D-day, it was interesting to watch a big old cruiser pull up about a half a mile off the beach and start blasting away at enemy positions on the island with their big guns. This went on and on for days. They laid their shells just out in front of our battle lines twenty four hours a day! The Japanese soldiers didn't have a chance to set down and have a sip of sake or anything else with thousands of shells exploding around them. Within a short time, the pounding completely demoralized the enemy.

We could feel the concussions from the distance and the unrelenting noise was really something to hear! All we could think about were those poor sailors aboard the ships who had to put up with the pounding vibrations and blasting sounds, as sleep or rest had to be impossible. There is a good book containing details of this written by James Fahey entitled "The Pacific War Dairy". He was a sailor just like me, but with a completely different perspective as a battle ship swabby. Some of our more enterprising boat crews would tie up to the stern of these big ships and go aboard with a box of souvenirs we had just picked up off of the beach or from destroyed towns. These guys would line up to pay anything for something that looked oriental! They especially liked Japanese money because they could mail it home and impress their friends and family. The poor guys didn't have any place to spend their money, so we helped them out whenever we could.

Our Atrocious Enemy ~ Read this, It's important

By Bob Kline, ~ Milt's Shipmate

The following article by our highly respected USS Rocky Mount historian is not for the faint hearted. But it is a story that should be told. As the English poet Samuel Taylor Coleridge wrote in 1831 "If men could learn from history, what lessons it might teach us!" In preparing this article, I consulted the following sources: Saipan; Suicide Island, by Guy Gabaldon, The Other Nuremberg, by Arnold Brachman; The Rape of Nanking, by Iris Chang, and Japanese War Crimes – Murder Under the Sun, on an A & E videotape.

One may question why, after more than a half-century has passed, we should discuss the horrible massacres in the Pacific during WWII. Some people say, "Don't look back." But a wise man once said, "Those who cannot remember the past are condemned to repeat it." Very few of us, while we were aboard the Rocky Mount, were aware of the atrocities being committed by our enemy. On the other hand, records of Hitler's behavior and the horrible holocaust in Europe fill hundreds of books, are preserved on file, and are on display in a national museum. They tell a story that should never be forgotten. But there are other stories that may too easily be forgotten.

In the 1980s on my first visit to the Japanese war areas, I received firsthand accounts of some Japanese wartime atrocities. On a visit to Guam on June 6, 1984, I talked to the Governor of Guam about his WWII memories. He was twelve

years old when the Japanese invaded his home island. The Japanese caught a classmate of his; he had been a runner for Guam's underground. The boy was sentenced to death. The Japanese emptied the entire school and forced every child to watch his execution. That twelve-year-old boy was shot to death in front of his young friends.

Once when I was shopping in Manila, an elderly shopkeeper asked me, "You a MacArthur man?" I said yes. She told me a horrible story about the Japanese storming the Manila hospital, where they unmercifully gouged out the eyes of babies and threw them against the wall.

In several small villages in Luzon, in the Philippines, some forty years after the war had ended, several natives told me about the treatment they and their families received from the

Japanese. Never forgotten was the Bataan Death March; the ten-day, 75 mile killing walk to POW cages in northern Luzon. They told me that Japanese soldiers took delight in watching more than 10,000 American and Filipino soldiers die, many of whom the Japanese simply bayoneted to death in the course of that horrendous march. Their Japanese captors especially hated downed American pilots; they were called "American Devils." Many captured pilots were tied to operating tables. Then Japanese doctors and medical students performed operations, without benefit of anesthesia, to remove parts of their bodies. While victims were screaming, "Kill me, kill me". Japanese soldiers seated in the gallery, drinking sake and eating rice balls, were jokingly making bets on how long it would take before the victim's unconsciousness would set in. A retired Japanese physician recently admitted that he learned more about human anatomy
through that barbarous practice than he ever did in medical school.

For Americans, our war with Japan started shortly after December 7, 1941. But there had been fighting in Asia long before that date. On December 13, 1937, Nanking, then a capital of Nationalist China, fell to the Japanese. It was there that one of the most brutal massacres in the history of mankind took place. The Japanese not only totally burned the city of Nanking, they also systematically raped, tortured, and murdered more than 300,000 Chinese civilians. The deaths in that city alone far exceeded the combined death toll of 210,000 from the atomic blasts at Hiroshima and Nagasaki. But in some Japanese prison camps, such atrocities did not occur. A friend of our family was an Army nurse who was captured at Corregidor in the Philippines. She was sent to a prison camp where she "was treated like a lady". Those horrible atrocities did not happen everywhere, only where military leaders permitted them. But, of course, they should not have happened anywhere.

Guy Gabaldon, in his book Saipan: Suicide Island, reports that when General Saito and Admiral Naguno committed suicide on July 9, 1944, many Japanese soldiers decapitated their best friends and buddies in a vast suicide pact. Standing in a row, the first man would kneel. Then the man behind him, using a mighty ceremonial sword, would behead him. Rather than surrender, this was the honorable thing to do. And so it went down the line. We on the RM were anchored offshore at the time. Little did we realize what was going on nearby.

I could go on and on reporting other atrocious actions of the Japanese army, but enough said. At the Tokyo War Crimes Trials, 28 high-ranking "Class A' war criminals were tried. Only seven were sentenced to death by hanging. Most others were sentenced to prison, but were subsequently paroled.

Despite all those horrible inhuman actions by our enemy, we must not forget that many Japanese-Americans fought in the US Army. As a unit they compiled a superb record for courage and endurance in the European Theater during WWII. So let us not ever blame an entire race or nationality for the actions of some individuals.

And yet, it is an odd and lamentable fact that throughout my travels in the Pacific area in recent years, whenever I discussed WWII events with Japanese citizens, not one of them professed to know anything about atrocities committed by their side. Instead, their standard question to me was this:

"Why did you bomb our cities?"

Robert Kline

Strike up the band

Our Ships Band ~ A letter from the following "Army shipmate" (there weren't many soldiers aboard) ~ Fred Crossland

While our ship was in Leyte Gulf waiting to invade Japan one Of the guys come up with a clarinet and another with a small Trap drum and they started playing polkas every night in the Mess hall. They were really good. It wasn't very long before someone came up with another instrument and then another. I don't remember how I got involved but I remember taking one of our LVCP' boats over to a cruiser (I think) and this guy went aboard and the next thing I knew they were lowering this beat up old piano down into my boat and we soon had it aboard our ship. They fixed up the piano and added some more instruments until we had a full band (Of sorts) Complete with dancing girls (guys with mops for hair) – You will never believe how good they were.

June 28, 2002

Dear Milt,

Thanks for your letter of June 6. I do indeed remember several occasions when we met and spoke at Rocky Mount Reunions. Your request for information about the RM (U.S.S. Rocky Mount) brought back memories, and I'll do my best to provide you with additional background.

First of all, it should be remembered that I was a member of a small U.S. Army Signal Corps Detachment assigned to the RM. We came aboard at commissioning and were considered part of ship's company. Thus, the RM band (someone once called "The Rocketeers") represented cooperation between the services. I was the only Army man among the musicians, but other Army men worked on the sound system, served as writers for shows, and sang.

Your recollection of the origins of the band is probably correct. I'm not sure at what point I became involved, but I think there were only four or five members at the time. I had been playing organ (a terrible little green thing that required continuous foot peddling) as a volunteer for the Chaplain's services and that probably brought me to someone's attention. I should make it clear at the outset that I was the only band member who previously played professionally. All the other band members either were rank amateurs who could barely read music, if at all, or earlier had some experience as members of high school marching bands. I started studying the piano at age five, and throughout the northeast while completing high school and college. My professional name was "Dan Raynor" and I was a regular member of Local 802, the New York unit of the American Federation of Musicians. Upon entering the Army I broke up my band (then consisting of 12 musicians, a girl vocalist, and a band boy or gofer), sold my library to MCA (then just a booking agency), coached a band of 4-F's MCA put together, and ended my musical career. In the Army I chose not to pursue an entertainer option, but joined the Signal Corps for

training Cryptanalysis and intelligence. Aboard the RM my
rank was Staff Sergeant.

Now back to the RM. Once I agreed to take the lead, several
amateur musicians began to show up and before long, we
had something like 14 or 15 in the group: four woodwinds, at
least six brasses, and four rhythms. Where and how all
those men managed to get their instruments sent to them
somewhere out in the Pacific remains a mystery to me. But
we had no music! So in my "spare time" in the Code Room I
wrote arrangements, orchestrating all the parts. Obviously I
had to keep everything simple to accommodate the minimum

skills of several of the players.

Many people aboard the ship contributed valuable services. Carpenters made music stands. Electricians created amplifiers and light for the music stands. Printers made up blank lined music paper for my arrangements. Throughout the ship, crew members voluntarily switched watches so band members could be free at the same times for rehearsals and shows. It truly was a cooperative effort.

For several months I had to struggle with that terrible little green pump organ. Then some sort of deal was worked out by the chaplains of the RM and another ship nearby (I thought I remember someone saying it was the battleship Pennsylvania, but I could be wrong) saying we could have their somewhat damaged piano if RM could provide the movers. That is the episode you recalled. Once we got it aboard the RM, we went to work on it. Carpenters repaired (as best they could) the sounding board. Electricians wired it for sound. I tuned it as best I could with a pair of borrowed pliers. It wasn't great, but at least somewhat better than that green pump organ.

I am not too clear about the time frame for all of this, but we probably got the salvaged piano sometime early in 1945. In June 1945 several of us headed back to the States for leave (my one and only) before the anticipated invasion of Japan. The war ended before I could return to the RM, and so ends that part of the story. I have no idea what happened to the band equipment or all the music (some of it originals) I had written and arranged.

To the best of my knowledge, no member of the RM band subsequently pursued a musical career. I went to graduate school (earned a Ph.D. in history at New York University), and ultimately became a professor and dean at that University. In 1964 I was invited to join the Ford Foundation with responsibility for grant programs in higher education throughout the country. I retired in 1981. I still play piano and keyboard occasionally, but for pleasure only.

Good luck with your own writing chore. It was a pleasure hearing from you, and I wish you well now and always.

Good Wishes, Fred

August 27, 1945
Friday, 6 PM
Philippines

Dear Mom,

I just finished eating chow a few minutes ago and am sitting high up on the top deck of the ship, I work up here so I keep all my gear up here, I sleep in a hammock up here too, its nice and cool and quiet.

I received your letter dated Aug 14, a couple days ago but haven't had much time for writing, it seems I owe a letter to every one I know.

Everything is still the same as in my last letter, I'm just putting in time, waiting for something to break, I get more homesick everyday but that's nothing unusual out here, all the older fellows with the most points are all set to leave for the states.

I can see a rain coming this way, its about ten miles off so there's no hurry, I can see all kinds of ships in all

274

directions and there, full of men wanting to come home, I'd hate to have to be the one in charge of this mess.

Don't worry about my boxing to morrow night will be my last fight, I just wanted to know just what I could and couldn't do, its been alot of fun and good experince.

You sound as every thing at home is oky, tell Freddie and every one hello for me. it is to bad you have to work but thats life for you, if I had you as a dependant it would mean ten more points toward coming home you good.

That rain went the other way so I'll close and try to write to dad before I gets to dark. Write lots and maybe it won't be to long before I'll be able to come home.

As Ever
Milton

Milton A. Shea
☓xxxx
⸤arks

The Last Reunion (So Sad)

In October 2004 was the last official reunion of the Rocky
Mount crew, we met in Fort Laterdale, Florida. There were
about thirty sailors left from the original seven hundred. They
were from all over the country and a great time was had by
all, but at the same time it was so sad to know that this would
be the last time that we would ever be together on this earth.
Over the years we have become very good friends. But now,
it was a final hoorah in every sense of the word. Instead of
rifles and bombs we were armed with wheel chairs, canes
and walkers.

When I joined up, I had just turned eighteen and most of my
shipmates were five to ten years older than me, now I am
eighty and they are really, really old. There were many wives
of departed sailors that attended with tears in their eyes.
They were wonderful ladies and had become a very important
part of our group and we loved them all very much. One of
our major problems was that we couldn't remember names or
our room numbers and were not sure of our flight or gate

numbers either. We took a roll call about every hour we all screamed with laughter with a tear in our eye.

Now Hear This ~

Our Memorial
For all of those of us that are still around, I'm sure that we can
speak for all of our departed shipmates. We all are so appreciative of the great effort put forth by those who created such a dynamic and fitting memorial in Washington DC.
Though we may have passed on ~ our spirit will remain with you forever.
As you stand there and view the monument, you will feel our presence next to you.

A final Word or Epilogue

As I bring this "little piece of work" to an end, I feel I should say something very profound and eloquent to describe what

277

the World War II experience has meant to me, but I just can't find the words. It was just too all encompassing and important in my life experiences. No one statement or expression can express the meaning of something so horrendous. Someone once said that "We create our own hell right here on earth". The word "Hell" means many different things to different people but to see and feel what I and millions of other young boys experienced in World War Two created a new meaning for the word. Some how we must try to control those that trade the lives of our youth for their own personal agenda.

You try to put it out of your mind and not think about it. But it is incumbent upon each of us to always be alert and to be responsible for the direction our life is taking us. The world of international power and politics is so complex that there has never been a way to stop or control those who have their own agenda. We do not learn from our mistakes, as history has proven. The opportunity to satisfy personal greed and ego is always there. To fight a war of economics that may bring starvation to millions is one thing, but to use the blood and excruciating pain of our productive youth simply to satisfy the needs of our leaders is just plain stupid! But I don't think I can do anything about it, except perhaps pray a lot.

I really enjoyed my association with those at my side during this traumatic drama, and through them, I am a better man today. So, to those shipmates who stood behind the wheel of those little wooden boats when they hit the beaches and felt the TEARS from the constant SALTWATER in their eyes, my heart goes out to you, and I'm proud to be one of you and wish you a safe harbor. ~ War is Hell.

Cheers, Hollywood

Milton Alexander Rhea,

Boatswains Mate 2nd Class (during the war)

The Sailor's Hymn

Eternal Father, strong to save

Whose arm does bind the restless wave?

Who bids the mighty ocean deep?

Its own appointed limits keep.

O hear us when we cry to Thee

For those in peril on the sea.

Eternal Father, whose strong word

The winds and waves submissive heard.
Who walked upon the foaming deep
And calm amid the storm did sleep.
O hear us when we cry to Thee
For those in peril on the sea

Eternal Father, who did pray
Upon the waters dark and gray,
Who bade their angry tumult cease
And gave for wild confusion peace.
O hear us when we cry to Thee
For those in peril on the sea.

Eternal Father, hear our prayer
For friends and shipmates everywhere.
Among those spared we pray you'll count
All those who served on "Rocky Mount"
These memories we will all hold dear
Until we meet again, some where, some year.

ISBN 141201716-5

Edwards Brothers Malloy
Oxnard, CA USA
April 24, 2014